The Best of Virginia City

AND THE

Comstock

by L.J. ETTINGER

DEDICATION

This book is dedicated to Hugh A. Shamberger (1900-1992):
a Nevada historian and pioneer in Nevada water resources.
Hugh was an extraordinary man, father and public servant.

And a special thanks to Ann, Hugh's daughter and my wife,
for all her help, patience and expertise in the preparation of this book.

ABOUT THE AUTHOR

LEN ETTINGER is a registered geologist and licensed attorney in the state of Idaho. He has a B.S. and M.S. in mining geology from the University of Arizona and Juris Doctor from the University of California at Los Angeles. He has worked as a staff and consulting exploration geologist and project coordinator for various companies in the western United States and internationally for more than 30 years. A Nevada resident since 1984, he has lived in the Virginia City area since 1991.

•

Cover illustration by Virginia City artist Dan Heath
—*a marriage of the past and the present*—

Typesetting, layout and design by Ann Ettinger
—*a pleasurable challenge*—

•

ISBN 0-9614840-5-5

Published by L.J. Ettinger
1991 Saddleback Road
Reno, Nevada 89511
(702) 847-9303
Printed in the U.S.A.

FOREWORD

Over the years, Virginia City and the Comstock Lode have been the subject of considerable study. In this work, Len Ettinger contributes to our understanding of the era, chronicling in a popular vein the development of the mines, the manner in which they were financed, and the personalities involved. The saga of the Sutro Tunnel, the connection of the Virginia and Truckee Railroad with the history of the Lode and the historic fire of October 26, 1875 are also chronicled. For those seeking a brief guide to the Comstock supplemented by maps, photos and anecdotal accounts of life as it was during the boom years, this book is the best to come off the presses in recent years.

—Phillip I. Earl
Nevada Historical Society

TABLE OF CONTENTS

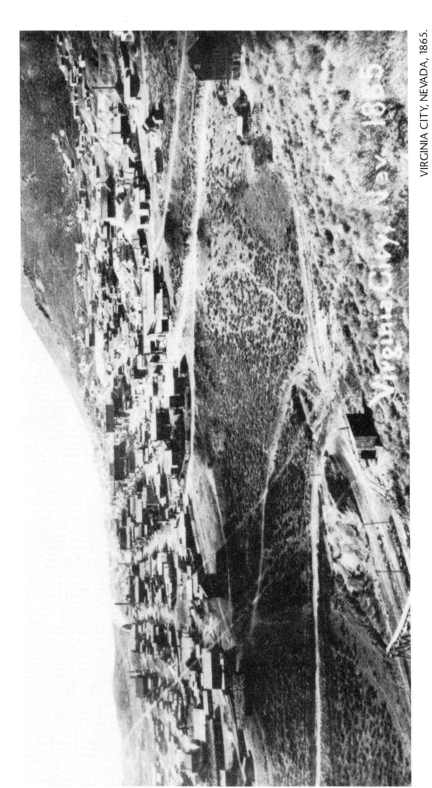

VIRGINIA CITY, NEVADA, 1865.
Courtesy of Nevada Historical Society.

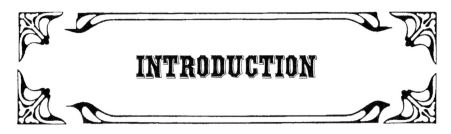

INTRODUCTION

THE COMSTOCK LODE, discovered in 1859, would produce $500 million in silver and gold over the next 75 years, and set in motion a series of events that would help shape the history of the western United States. The Comstock would be the first silver mining camp in the country and Virginia City would grow from a camp of several hundred to a city with a population of 15,000 by 1863.

In 1860 San Francisco had a population of 52,000. Nearly all profits from the Comstock's early years would be invested in San Francisco real estate, including the erection of fine buildings. California was the source of nearly all supplies coming into the Comstock until completion of the transcontinental railroad in 1869.

Discovery of the Comstock 10 years after discovery of gold in the Mother Lode of California encouraged prospectors to look for mines throughout the west. Mining was the economic factor that created the Nevada Territory, carved out of the Utah Territory in 1861, and then supported statehood for Nevada in 1864. Mining would be Nevada's main industry for some 30 years.

The Comstock contributed more than $50 million in silver and gold to the federal government during the Civil War (1861 to 1865).

Mining methods were primitive in 1859. The Ophir and Mexican claims hired Mexican miners who used rawhide buckets supported on their backs by a strap that passed across their foreheads. Ascent and descent into the mines was by means of logs with steps cut in them. Pumping water out of mine shafts was by hand. Milling the ore was by use of the arrastra (a primitive rock crushing device).

Within a year new mining and milling methods were developed to meet the existing conditions which included broken ground, hot rocks and water (up to 170°F at the deeper levels) and poor ventilation. The broken ground encountered was shored up by the new square set system invented by Philip Deidesheimer. Donkey engines using steam power were brought in for hoisting and pumping. Stamp mills were built and the "Washoe Process" was initiated to recover the silver and gold from the rich ores.

The first flat iron wire rope was made in 1863.

Blasting techniques evolved to the use of giant powder cartridges. Ventilation and pumping techniques also evolved with larger steam engines and installation of giant Cornish pumps.

The Sutro Tunnel, designed to drain water from the mines, would be one of the longest of its time.

New methods of mass production of lumber were developed including design and construction of the V-flume in 1866. The design and engineering of the Virginia City water transport system, constructed in 1873 and spanning some 25 miles from its source near Lake Tahoe, was a marvel of its time. It used an inverted siphon design that covered a vertical elevation of more than 1,600 feet.

Today Virginia City is one of the best preserved old mining towns that can be found anywhere.

♦

VIRGINIA CITY IN 1865, LOOKING DOWN SIX MILE CANYON.
Courtesy of Nevada Historical Society.

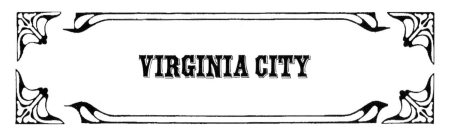

VIRGINIA CITY

ONE OF THE MOST FAMOUS mining camps in the world, Virginia City was established in 1859 after the discovery of the Comstock Lode. The mining camp near the strike was first called Pleasant Hills and Mount Pleasant Point, then Ophir, and finally named Virginia by the early prospectors in honor of James "Old Virginny" Finney because of his discovery, his knowledge of placers below what would later be the Ophir Mine, and his location of the first quartz mining claim on the Comstock.

Virginia City, county seat of Storey County, is on the east side of the Virginia Range just below Mount Davidson at an elevation of 6,220 feet. Today Virginia City is within the Comstock District, a national landmark since 1961, and is a year-round international tourist attraction with a population of about 700.

In the fall of 1859, Virginia City had an initial population of between 200 and 300. After word of the Comstock discovery in early 1860, perhaps 10,000 rushed to the Comstock, many from the California goldfields. About 4,000 remained in the area; 2,345 in Virginia City (868 dwellings), and the rest in Gold Hill and vicinity. The political ramifications resulted in the creation of the Nevada Territory, carved from Utah Territory, by President Buchanan on March 2, 1861.

The population remained about 4,000 through 1862. Samuel Clemens arrived in late 1862, worked as a reporter for the *Territorial Enterprise* for about 21 months, and left as Mark Twain. During this period construction of the old Geiger Grade Toll Road was started and in partial use by the end of the year. This road linked Virginia City with emigrant trails and supply routes that crossed the Truckee River at the site that would become Reno in 1868. Organization of the San Francisco Stock Exchange Board, the first mining exchange in the United States, also occurred in 1862.

By 1863, mining successes and promotion brought the Virginia City and vicinity population to some 15,000. Homes, business buildings and office blocks were built; gas and sewer pipes were laid in the principal main streets. Daily stages brought in all the luxuries of the Bay Area. The town was made up of two classes of people, each of which kept its own place and went its way without interference from the other. Seventy-five stamp-amalgamation mills were operating in the region: 19 in Virginia City and in Six and Seven Mile canyons belc N, 35 in Gold Canyon from Gold Hill to Dayton, 12 on the Carson River, and nine in Washoe Valley.

The Comstock brought enough people, money and politicians to the area that on October 31, 1864, Nevada was admitted as the 36th state. Economic slow-down saw 10,000 leave the area, many for other mining camps, dropping the area population to about 4,000 in 1865. Virginia City population increased to about 11,000 by 1868. The Yellow Jacket Mine fire occurred in 1869. The construction of the Virginia and Truckee Railroad between Virginia City and Carson City was begun in 1869 and completed in 1870. The rail line between Carson City and Reno was completed on August 24, 1872, connecting with the existing Central Pacific Railroad. This pretty much ended the wagon freight business over the Sierra and to Virginia City.

The increased mining operations and population between 1859 and 1870 expended the available local water from natural springs and mine tunnels to the west of town. In 1870, plans were made to bring water to the Comstock from Marlette Lake high in the Sierra near Lake Tahoe, down the east slope of the Sierra, and across Washoe Valley using an inverted siphon system. This was completed in August 1873 and, now modernized, is the source of Virginia City water today.

Between 1873 and 1874, as the result of the discovery of the Bonanza ore body in the Consolidated Virginia Mine which extended into the California Mine, the population of the area exploded to 25,000 in Virginia City and 5,000 in Gold Hill.

On October 26, 1875, just after 6 a.m., a fire, probably started from a wood stove, destroyed most of Virginia City, burning an area of about one square mile.

During 1876 Virginia City was rebuilding and supported a regional population of 23,000. The Irish predominated in Virginia City and the Cornish in Gold Hill.

The third line vertical shafts were being sunk east of town (evidenced by the large mine dumps) to intersect the Comstock Lode at depths of 2,500 to 4,500 feet.

Of the 135 Comstock mines quoted in the San Francisco Stock Exchanges in 1876, only three, the Consolidated Virginia, the California, and the Belcher, were paying dividends. All the others were levying assessments.

The decline of Virginia City began in 1877 as hard times hit the Comstock and discoveries were made in other mining districts in Nevada and California. In 1880 there were about 11,000 people and 1,200 buildings in Virginia City of which 92 were made of brick. Most of the mines closed after the panic of 1893 and by 1900 the population of Virginia City had dwindled to 2,700, continuing downward to about 500 in 1930. In 1980, the census showed 1,503 living in the Virginia City-Gold Hill area.

As an epilog it can probably be said that the Comstock produced 29 millionaires in an environment where more than 1,000 mining companies were formed, of which only 19 ever paid dividends. More money was lost in the essentially unregulated stock market through assessments and stock manipulations than was ever produced in gold and silver.

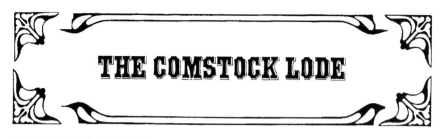

THE COMSTOCK LODE

THE COMSTOCK LODE is one of the great precious metal mining districts in the world. Named after Henry Comstock, who was an early arrival on the scene of the initial discovery, the district would produce about $500 million in gold and silver, and would shape the early history of the West.

A few colors of gold found in a stream near Dayton by a young man on his way to the California goldfields in 1850 led to the discovery of the Comstock Lode. Gravels were placered up Gold Canyon and Six Mile Canyon for nine years until, in early 1859, two groups of placer miners finally reached the Lode outcrops rich in gold and silver—one group at the southern end at the head of Gold Canyon and the other group about one mile to the north at the head of Six Mile Canyon. Word of high grade gold and silver started a rush from California, the East Coast and the rest of the world.

The earliest mining was by hand and led to new near-surface discoveries of rich gold and silver ore. Promoters bought into the properties, formed companies, and soon many were selling stock in San Francisco. With investment capital came major underground operations, the construction of large stamp amalgamation mills and the building of Virginia City, Gold Hill and other communities.

The Comstock Lode occurs within a north trending, 50° east dipping, fault zone some three miles long which splits into two branches at its southern end and at least three branches at its northern end. The Lode ranges in width from 200 to 1,000 feet at the surface, narrowing to an average width of 100 feet at a depth of 500 feet. The mineralized zone includes gold and silver in crushed quartz (see cross section on page 16).

Mining proved difficult because of the crushed and sheared ground in and near the fault zone, and the great quantities of hot water encountered at depth. The bad ground required creation of a new mining method—square set stoping—and the use of great quantities of timber. Hot water (up to 170°F) required pumping as the mines got deeper, along with a hotter work environment (100 to 125°F). The water problem was tackled by Adolph Sutro and resulted in the construction of the Sutro Tunnel. Ventilation of the mines was accomplished using automatic air circulation through shafts standing at different elevations.

By 1865, the mine workings reached about 600 feet in depth. Hot water, bad ground and ventilation were problems that proved very costly to overcome. Mining continued and during 1866, one mine after another found new and almost unexpected ore bodies, with continued progress in 1867 and 1868. The years 1869 through 1871 were down years, followed by a stock market boom in 1872.

In early 1873, the Consolidated Virginia and California Bonanza was encountered 1,200 feet vertically below the surface under the heart of Virginia City. The bonanza extended to the 1,650 foot level and was mined out by 1882. A total of 1.4 million tons of gold-silver ore was mined, yielding $105 million, from which $74 million was paid in dividends.

These were the Comstock glory years.

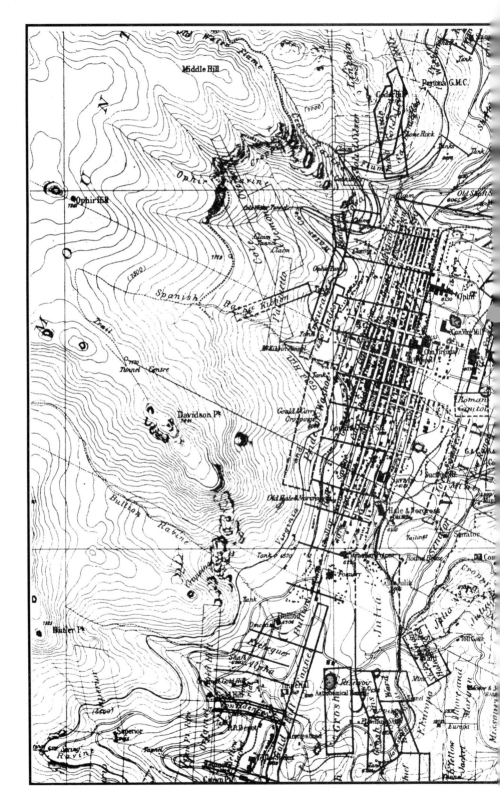

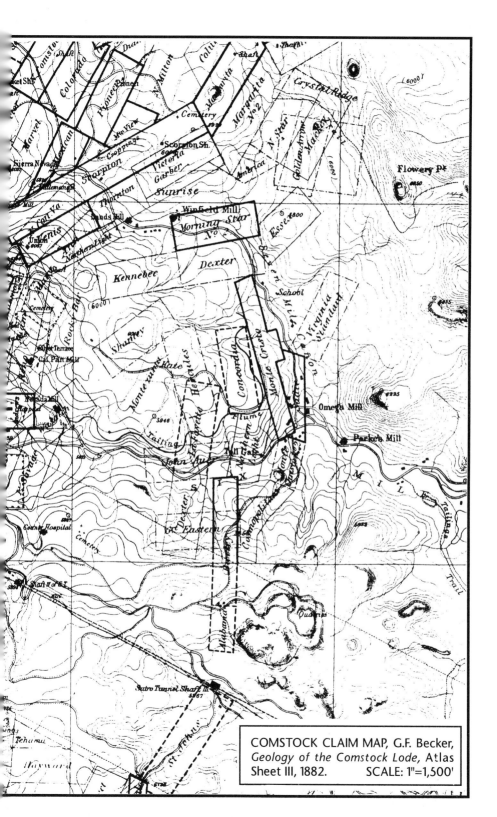

COMSTOCK CLAIM MAP, G.F. Becker,
Geology of the Comstock Lode, Atlas
Sheet III, 1882.   SCALE: 1"=1,500'

Adolph Sutro proposed a drainage tunnel to dewater the mines in 1864. Started in 1869 and completed in 1878, the four mile long Sutro Tunnel connected with the Savage Shaft, with a 4,403 north lateral reaching the Union Shaft and a 8,423 south lateral to the Alta Shaft. The tunnel drained 3.5 to 4 million gallons of water daily, but reached the mine workings too late to be of real value because the mines were then working deeper than the tunnel elevation.

By 1880, the glory of the Comstock had passed. Not only was it finished as a profitable mining region, but most of the ambitious, energetic men had departed or were soon to leave.

After 1880, the major mines continued deep exploration to 3,000 vertical feet below the surface without discovery of any new bonanzas. The water problems, the hot temperatures of rock and water, and the expenditure of $40 million were all reasons why work ceased in 1886 and the mines were allowed to flood. The companies now turned to mining near-surface low-grade ore. In 1896 the new cyanide process was brought to the Comstock, replacing the mercury amalgamation process. In the following years millions of tons of tailings, mine dumps and near-surface low-grade deposits were worked.

Production of gold and silver from the Comstock Lode can be divided into four periods. The first, 1859 to 1865, as follows: 1859—about $275,000; 1860—about $1 million; 1861—about $2.5 million; 1862—about $6 million; 1863—about $12.4 million; 1864 and 1865—about $16 million each year, totalling a little over $50 million for the first six years. However, the Comstock mines as a whole failed to show a profit. The assessments and expenditures exceeded the dividends. "The high cost of operations, wasteful and extravagant management, and millions uselessly and foolishly expended in exploration work, together with vexatious and costly litigation, had consumed that splendid output."

In the second period, production between 1866 and 1870 was about $60 million, yielding a net profit of about $5 million. During the third period, between 1871 and 1881, the Comstock mines produced $320 million from ore and tailings and paid $147 million in dividends. The assessments levied and expenditures by private companies and individuals was more than $92 million, leaving a net profit of $55 million. In the fourth and last period, between 1882 and the present, production has been about $80 million.

Related to the Comstock mining activities was regional timber harvest and the use of mercury and cyanide in ore processing. Between 1860 and 1880, the Sierra was devasted for a length of 60 miles to provide 600 million feet of lumber that went into the Comstock mines, and two million cords of firewood consumed by the mines and mills.

Amalgamation uses mercury to recover gold. It is estimated that the early milling methods resulted in tailings losses of 25 percent of the gold and silver values, along with some 14 million pounds of mercury lost in Gold Canyon and Six Mile Canyon, at least part of which worked down into the Carson River. After 1900, cyanide was used to recover gold and large quantities of spent cyanide were deposited with the mill tailings. However, with time, cyanide becomes neutralized and not an environmental problem.

Although much low grade gold and silver rock remains, today it is doubtful whether it will ever be mined in the Virginia City-Gold Hill area because of the proximity to these populated areas and the related environmental concerns.

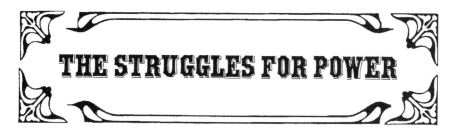

THE STRUGGLES FOR POWER

A HISTORY OF THE COMSTOCK would not be complete without a background of the personalities that fought for power over the richest silver-gold mining district that the world had known. The main players were Adolph Sutro and two groups, the "Bank Crowd" and the "Silver Kings."

By 1863 there were 15,000 people in Virginia City and construction along the Comstock had reached over $12 million. Virginia City needed a bank and that need was met by the new Arnold & Blauvelt Bank.

THE BANK CROWD

A year later William Ralston of San Francisco sent William Sharon to the Comstock to buy out the Arnold & Blauvelt Bank and replaced it with the Bank of California.

The timing was right for the Bank of California. Stocks were low and money was needed to develop the Lode. Sharon, now managing the Virginia City branch of the Bank of California, loaned money at two percent per month, undercutting other lenders whose rates were five percent.

Borrowers, mainly mine and mill owners, stood in line, giving their mines and mills as security for their loans. A decline in ore yield during 1865-66 reduced the independent milling operations substantially and loans could not be repaid. The bank foreclosed, taking the mills.

Now greedy minds went to work and a power play was formulated. Early in 1867 the Union Mill and Mining Company was incorporated to take over the seven mills the bank had repossessed. The charter members, to be known as the "Bank Ring" or "Bank Crowd," were D.O. Mills, William Sharon, W.C. Ralston, Alvinza Hayward, Thomas Sunderland, Charles Bonner, Thomas Bell and William E. Barron, the same men who controlled the Bank of California.

Within two years 10 more mills were repossessed and the Union Mill and Mining Company was in a position to control almost every producing mine on the Comstock. They were in a position to freeze out independent mill owners and control whether stockholders of their mines were paid dividends or were assessed. This could be accomplished by mixing waste rock with the ore to dilute its value to only cover the expense of mining and milling.

The "Bank Crowd" could also manipulate the price of stock with their knowledge of new ore bodies discovered in their mines and the timing of announcements of the new discoveries. During the 1860s stock transactions were essentially unregulated and they could buy and sell at will, making enormous profits.

During this period Sharon became a director of the Virginia and Gold Hill Water Company.

ADOLPH SUTRO

Adolph Sutro was a self-made German immigrant who came to the Comstock in 1860 from San Francisco where he owned several stores that specialized in tobacco. In 1862 he built a steam-powered ore reducing mill near Dayton which burned down in late 1863.

The year 1863 was a boom year for the Comstock and ore bodies were being mined to 500 feet in depth. It was thought that the Lode would go on in depth "forever." There were problems, however. The rock within the Lode was crushed and required square set timbering and great quantities of warm water were encountered.

Sutro proposed a drainage tunnel to de-water all the mines to a vertical depth of 1,400 feet and by 1864, his tunnel idea was gaining support. With support of most of the mine owners, in early 1875 Sutro received an exclusive franchise from the state of Nevada to construct and operate a drainage tunnel for 50 years.

In July 1866 the U.S. Congress passed the Sutro Tunnel Act empowering Sutro to purchase federal land necessary for his tunnel and granting him necessary right-of-ways. Sutro promoted his tunnel and by May 1867 he had stock subscriptions of $600,000 from 11 of the Comstock mining companies.

Sutro was feeling the "urges" of power and in one of his prospectuses he prophesized that, once his tunnel was completed, he and his investors would control the Comstock; that the majority of the populations of Virginia City and Gold Hill would shift to his new town of Sutro at the mouth of the tunnel near Dayton; that all ore would be transported through his tunnel to his mills along the Carson River; and that all timber and freight for the mines would be transported through his tunnel.

When the "Bank Crowd" learned of Sutro's prophesy they were outraged. This was probably the reason why the Union Mill and Mining Company was created and also probably why William Sharon incorporated the Virginia & Truckee Railroad Company in 1867.

In order to block construction of the Sutro Tunnel, the "Bank Crowd," along with their Union Mill & Mining Company, exerted pressure so that the $600,000 in Sutro Tunnel stock subscriptions was never ratified and Sutro was forced to look for new money.

The power struggle also became political both in Nevada and in Washington, D.C., which helped delay the Sutro Tunnel project for years.

Sutro ultimately completed his tunnel in 1879 and the laterals by 1888, but by then it was much too late to be of beneficial use to the Comstock.

THE SILVER KINGS

John Mackay and James Fair had been on the Comstock since 1860 and knew the Lode from one end to the other. Mackay would become superintendent of the Caledonia and then the Bullion mines and Fair was superintendent of the Ophir Mine in 1866.

Mackay and Fair joined forces to gain control of the Hale & Norcross Mine, a mine in which they recognized potential, which was controlled by the Union Mill & Mining Company. They needed more capital and approached two old friends, James Flood and William O'Brien, who were operating the Auction Lunch Saloon in San Francisco. They would be known as the "Silver Kings" or the "Firm."

With a capital of $220,000, their first attempt to take control of the Hale & Norcross in 1868 did not succeed. A few months later, when stock fell, the Mackay group was able to purchase enough to take control in 1869. A pending assessment was rescinded and the mine began to prosper and pay dividends. A new ore body was discovered in 1870 and dividends continued until 1872 when assessments were again levied.

During this time the "Silver Kings" fought Sutro's tunnel project and purchased Sharon's interest in the Virginia and Gold Hill Water Company.

Having made a million dollars with the Hale & Norcross Mine, the "Silver Kings" began looking for new ground to explore along the Comstock. In 1871, they began to quietly buy Consolidated Virginia & California stock, properties held by the "Bank Crowd" since 1867. These properties were located between the Ophir and Gould & Curry mines, both producers of ore over the past decade. Because of money problems the properties had only been explored to a depth of 500 feet. The "Silver Kings" believed they would find deeper ore. In early 1872 they took control for less than $50,000. The stock quickly rose tenfold because of the "Crown Point Bonanza Boom." Exploration continued through 1872 and on March 1, 1873 the top of the "Big Bonanza" ore body was encountered.

Money is power and in the next four years the "Big Bonanza" yielded 1.4 million tons of gold-silver ore totalling $105 million from which $74 million was paid in dividends.

Discovery of the "Big Bonanza" by the "Silver Kings" must have been a bitter pill for the "Bank Crowd" to swallow for they had earlier control of the property.

SLUGGING IT OUT

In 1872 both Sharon and Sutro ran for the U.S. Senate and both lost. Sutro would run and lose five times between 1872 and 1880. Sharon would run again in 1874 and be elected. Sharon bought the *Territorial Enterprise* in February 1874 to help his senatorial campaign, and owned it until his death on November 14, 1885. Sutro started his own newspaper, *The Daily Independent,* which remained in business for five months from June 1 to October 31, 1874.

Owning the Virginia and Truckee Railroad, the "Bank Crowd" was in a position to manipulate freight charges. The "Silver Kings" thought that their freight charges were too high and requested that the charges be reduced. When the V&T Railroad declined, Mackay responded that if freight charges weren't reduced immediately he would build his own railroad. Freight charges were quickly reduced to reasonably reflect services rendered.

In 1873 the "Bank Crowd" jumped into the lumber business forming the Carson & Tahoe Lumber and Fluming Company. By 1875 the "Silver Kings," with "Big Bonanza" money rolling in, formed the Pacific Wood, Lumber & Fluming Company.

The "Silver Kings" were building mills, and in January 1875 the new Consolidated Virginia 60-stamp mill, costing $300,000, was completed and began processing "Big Bonanza" ore at 260 tons per day. Later that year they began building a larger 80-stamp, 360 ton per day mill. In May of 1875 the "Silver Kings" incorporated the Nevada Bank with a capital of $5 million.

On August 26 of the same year the Bank of California failed, closing its doors. The next day William Ralston went for a swim in San Francisco Bay and his body was found washed ashore. This marked the end of the "Bank Crowd," and the "Silver Kings" now controlled the Comstock.

In 1880, Sutro sold his stock in the Sutro Tunnel Company and moved to San Francisco.

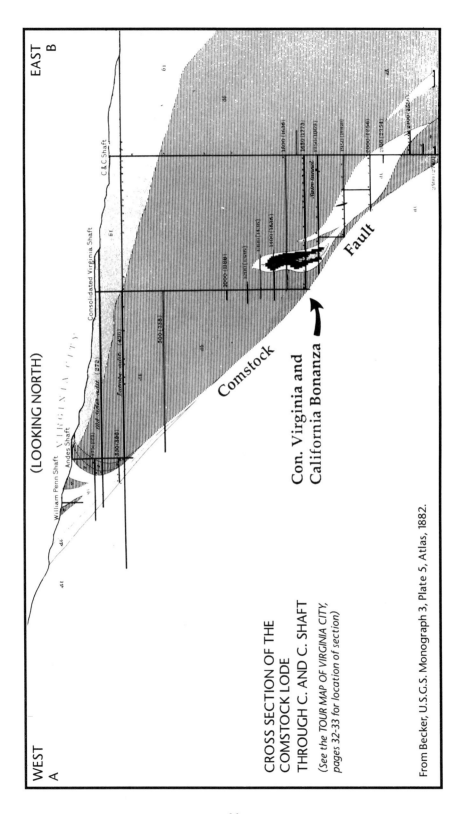

WEST
A

(LOOKING NORTH)

EAST
B

CROSS SECTION OF THE
COMSTOCK LODE
THROUGH C. AND C. SHAFT

*(See the TOUR MAP OF VIRGINIA CITY,
pages 32-33 for location of section)*

Con. Virginia and
California Bonanza

Comstock

Fault

William Penn Shaft

Andes Shaft

Consolidated Virginia Shaft

C & C Shaft

VIRGINIA CITY

From Becker, U.S.G.S. Monograph 3, Plate 5, Atlas, 1882.

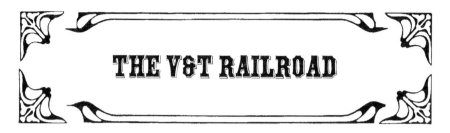

THE V&T RAILROAD

DISCOVERY OF THE COMSTOCK LODE in 1859 was one of the driving forces in development of the western United States. Over the next 20 years more than $300 million in gold and silver would be produced. Nevada would become the 36th state in 1864. San Francisco would become a major west coast city. The gold and silver mined would help finance the North in the Civil War. Trails would become wagon roads and the freight business would boom. The railroads would follow and railroad barons would become wealthy and powerful.

Fortunes would be made by mine owners, promoters, and businessmen from ore treatment, lumber, stock speculation, service industries including freight, saloons, gambling houses and banking.

The Comstock and Virginia City quickly developed, the word spread, and the rush was on. From the Mother Lode of California, from the east and from all parts of the world they came, hoping to make their fortunes.

Virginia City, built over the downward projection of the Comstock Lode, is at an elevation of 6,200 feet. The nearest water necessary to drive the ore reduction mills was the Carson River at an elevation of 4,600 feet, 10 miles south of Virginia City. In 1860, as the mines developed, only wagon trails served Virginia City and freight costs were high. The teamsters hauled ore from the mines to the Carson River, traveled to Carson City, Washoe City, and the Tahoe region, and then hauled freight and lumber on the return trip. From the Truckee River freight was hauled 21 miles to Virginia City over Geiger Grade.

PLANS TO CONSTRUCT A VIRGINIA CITY TO
CARSON CITY RAILROAD

Men with vision began to think about a rail line between Virginia City and Carson City and north to the Truckee River, where it was already known that the transcontinental railroad would pass. As early as 1860, Leonard Treadwell made application for a railroad franchise. It was chartered November 29, 1861, as the Virginia, Carson & Truckee Railroad Co., but the financing could not be raised and the project failed.

In 1862 there were 82 small mills along the Carson River and two more railroads were proposed. On December 20, 1862 a new charter was granted to other interests in the name of Virginia & Truckee Railroad Co. with three years to complete the project. On September 1, 1865, a second project started with the incorporation of the Virginia & Truckee River Railroad Co. These projects also failed.

At the same time the Bank of California, formed in 1864 in San Francisco, was headed by Darius Ogden Mills who was assisted by financial genius William C. Ralston. Soon after, the Bank of California opened a branch in Virginia City and Ralston appointed William Sharon as bank manager. Sharon had experienced a boom and bust career in California as a storekeeper and in real estate speculation. He was a calculating businessman and, by providing lower interest rate loans to the Comstock mines and mill owners, the bank was able to take over properties when financial difficulties were encountered. The bank gained control of seven Comstock mills, then transferred them to the Union Mill & Mining Company, whose shareholders, Mills, Ralston, Sharon and others, were also the shareholders of the bank.

THE TRANSCONTINENTAL RAILROAD

While Virginia City and the Comstock mines were struggling to get a railroad project off the ground, the Central Pacific Railroad transcontinental project was well underway. It's route was surveyed across the Sierra through what is now Reno and eastward along the Truckee River.

A transcontinental railroad was first proposed in the 1830s and brought to the attention of Congress in the mid-1840s. In 1853 the Pacific Railroad Surveys were authorized and five alternative routes proposed. The Civil War in 1861 stressed the need to unite California to the Union cause and on July 1, 1862, President Lincoln signed the Pacific Railroad Act. By contract the Union Pacific would lay track westward from Omaha, Nebraska and the Central Pacific would lay track eastward from Sacramento.

The contract between the U.S. government and the Central Pacific was signed on November 1, 1862, and construction started in Sacramento on January 8, 1863. It took nearly five years to cross the Sierra. The track reached Nevada on December 13, 1867, and Lake's Crossing on May 4, 1868. Myron Lake made an agreement with the Central Pacific to lay out a new townsite named Reno in honor of Jesse Lee Reno, a Union general killed September 1863 in the battle of South Mountain in the Civil War.

VIRGINIA AND TRUCKEE RAILROAD CO.

By 1867 the Union Milling & Mining Company was a self-contained monopoly which had consolidated all of the important independent operators on the Comstock. By necessity, Mills, Ralston and Sharon became mining men. Their biggest dilemma was the high cost of the teamster freight.

Low grade ores mined at greater depths were not worth the cost of teaming to the mills along the Carson River, nor was it economical to haul the firewood needed to feed the furnaces at the shaft heads on the return trip.

Mills driven by water power could reduce ore by one half the cost of those driven by steam fueled by expensive wood. Hauling ore to the Carson River by wagon cost $4 a ton and was subject to the condition of the roads in winter and early spring. A railroad hauling ore at $2 a ton would make a large volume of lower-grade ore available and profit the river mills now owned by the Union Mill & Mining Company. Wood costs would be cut from $29 to $21 per thousand feet, a savings of about $900,000 a year on overland freight. A railroad was the only answer, another link in the monopoly by which Sharon and the Bank of California would control and extract the profits from every activity in the Comstock.

Mills, Ralston and Sharon knew a Virginia City to Carson City railroad was feasible and necessary and past projects had folded because of lack of financing. Sharon also knew that he could build the railroad using public funds and still remain in control. With this in mind and to get the people of Carson City's attention, on May 8, 1867, Sharon incorporated the Virginia & Truckee Railroad Co. which was to be built from Gold Hill northerly through Virginia City and along Lousetown Creek to the Truckee River about 10 miles east of Lake's Crossing (Reno). Some of this old railroad grade can still be seen after leaving Highway 341 about a mile north on Lousetown Road.

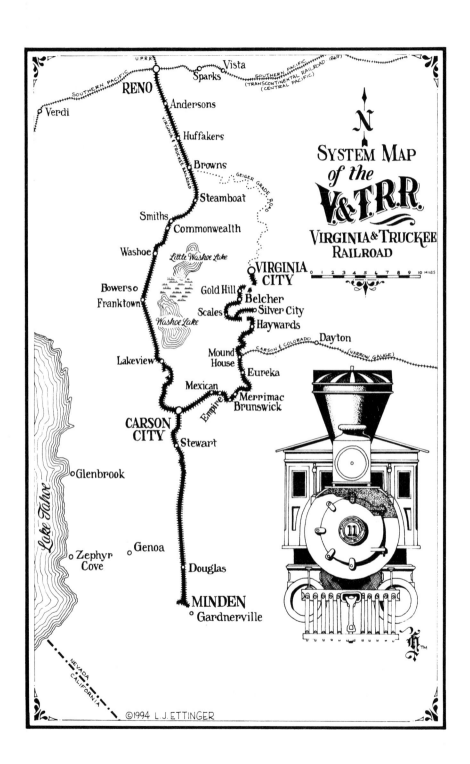

Vista

Sparks

RENO

U.P.R.R.

SOUTHERN PACIFIC (1869)
TRANSCONTINENTAL RAILROAD
(CENTRAL PACIFIC)

SOUTHERN PACIFIC

Verdi

Andersons

Huffakers

VIRGINIA & TRUCKEE RAILROAD

Browns

GEIGER GRADE ROAD

Steamboat

Smiths

Commonwealth

Washoe

Little Washoe Lake

VIRGINIA CITY

Bowers

Franktown

Gold Hill

Belcher

Silver City

Scales

Washoe Lake

Haywards

Dayton

Mound House

CARSON & COLORADO

(NARROW GAUGE)

Lakeview

Eureka

Mexican

Empire

Merrimac
Brunswick

CARSON CITY

Stewart

Glenbrook

Lake Tahoe

Genoa

Zephyr Cove

Douglas

MINDEN

Gardnerville

NEVADA
CALIFORNIA

SYSTEM MAP
of the
V.&T.R.R.
VIRGINIA & TRUCKEE
RAILROAD

0 1 2 3 4 5 6 7 8 9 10 MILES

11

©1994 L.J.ETTINGER

In September 1867, the route was surveyed and, as expected, the residents of Carson City and Washoe Valley rose up in protest that they were being by-passed. The protest continued when Sharon next envisioned a plan to build a strictly company railroad from Virginia City to the mills along the Carson River, ending at Empire. Thus the Virginia City & Carson River Railroad was born.

Afraid of being completely left isolated from a railroad, the protestors met with Sharon. An agreement was reached, and very quickly the people of Ormsby and Storey counties petitioned the legislature to authorize their counties to issue a total of $500,000 in county bonds to help finance the railroad from Virginia City to Carson City. Part of Sharon's sales pitch was the promise of largely increased taxes on the railroad that would go to the counties at an assessed value of $40,000 per mile.

As part of the overall agreement, the mines owned by Sharon would contribute $613,000, the Bank of California $1,500,000, and the mill owners who were not part of the Union Mill & Mining Company would raise an additional $387,000, with the promise that it would eventually be paid back in freight credits. Monies raised would total $3 million.

The Virginia City & Carson River Railroad was reorganized on March 2, 1868 with a capital of $3 million to build "the crookedest railway in the United States" (because of the railroad's torturous course and also to the manner in which it was financed) from Virginia City to Carson City.

Sharon quickly revised his plans by adding an additional 30 miles of railroad from Carson City north to the Truckee River to be constructed at a later date linking with the Central Pacific and the outside world. This would also put an end to the teamster monopoly. The Virginia City & Carson River Railroad became the Virginia & Truckee River Railroad, then shortened to the Virginia & Truckee Railroad—The V&T.

BUILDING THE RAILROAD — VIRGINIA CITY TO CARSON CITY

On January 9, 1869, William Sharon succeeded Thomas Sunderland as president of the Virginia & Truckee Railroad Company and mining surveyor Isaac James was given the job of surveying a route from Virginia City to the mills along the Carson River, a drop in elevation of about 1,600 feet. The route surveyed had a maximum grade of 2.2%, wrapping around the hills with a curvature equivalent to 17 complete circles in a distance of 13-1/2 miles. On Ferbruar 18, 1969 ground was broken two miles below Gold Hill on American Flat by a work gang of 40 men, which increased to 450 in April and 1,600 in June.

Experienced miners were hired to build the first three tunnels (of seven that would ultimately be constructed) which took five months to complete. Thirty-eight grading camps were established to house the mostly Chinese workers, many who came from working on the Central Pacific. Crown Point Ravine was crossed with an 93 foot high, 365 foot long trestle, completed on September 30, 1869.

The first three locomotives purchased were manufactured by Booth & Company of San Francisco. The "Lyon," "Ormsby," and "Storey" were hauled from Reno in pieces by wagon into Carson City on August 6th. On September 28, 1869 the first spike was driven by V&T superintendent H.M. Yerington. Two additional engines, the "Carson" and "Virginia," built by the Baldwin Locomotive Works, were hauled from Reno to Virginia City over Geiger Grade in early October 1869. The rails laid were rolled in Sheffield, England and carried by ship around the Horn. Ties were hewn from the forests around Lake Tahoe.

Soon after track laying began out of Carson City, the Chinese graders were run off the job by miners who feared the Chinese would challenge their jobs in the mines. Sharon assured the miners that no Chinese would be used in the mines and none would be used by the V&T north of the American Mine Hoisting Works.

In early November 1869, an assessment of $3.00 was levied on V&T stock subscriptions. The first regular train reached the Crown Point Trestle on November 12, and on December 21, 1869 scheduled trains were operating from Carson City to Gold Hill.

On January 29, 1870, the railroad was completed and the first passenger train, consisting of a combination baggage-passenger car, traveled from Carson City to the end of the line near the Gould and Curry Works at Virginia City, a distance of 21 miles. From ground breaking to scheduled operation took just over 11 months.

A ticket for the 2-1/2 hour ride from Virginia City to Carson City cost $2.00 and the ride from Virginia City to Gold Hill was 25 cents. Initially there was one scheduled passenger and four freight trains a day in each direction.

Rail transport brought an immediate reduction in the cost of moving ore from the mines to the mills along the Carson River. The cost savings of transporting lumber was one-third to one-half that which the teamsters charged. Two short branch lines, one two miles and the other one and a half miles long, were constructed in 1870 from Carson City to reach the end of the flumes carrying timber out of the Sierra for additional transport savings.

CONTINUING THE V&T FROM CARSON CITY TO RENO

During 1870, William Sharon waited for the people of Washoe County to demand that bonds be issued for continuing the V&T from Carson City to Reno. Nothing happened. In February 1871, Hill Beachey, a stage operator from Winnemucca and his associates were granted a right-of-way from Virginia City to Reno by the Nevada legislature. The route that was surveyed went north out of Virginia City and then partly paralleled present day Geiger Grade. By June construction began, some of which can still be seen to the north about one-fourth mile south of Geiger Summit on Highway 341.

Sharon could wait no longer. On July 1, 1871, he contracted to have a railroad bridge built across the Truckee River in Reno, where present day Holcomb Avenue meets the river. Construction began in early July and by July 22, a track connection had been made with the Central Pacific Railroad. By November 11, 1871, the line reached Steamboat Springs, and on August 24, 1872 the V&T operated its first train from Reno to Virginia City, a distance of 52 miles. Construction of the V&T's round house and machine shops commenced in Carson City. After the V&T arrived in Reno, almost overnight the business going to a dozen stages and hundreds of freight wagons was almost entirely diverted to the railroad.

THE BIG BONANZA

The Big Bonanza ore body was discovered in February 1873, and the railroad began earning $100,000 monthly profit from increased traffic. Freight carried by the V&T during the first six months of 1873 from the mines to the mills along the Carson River and to Carson City consisted of 112,044 tons of ore, 6,048 tons of tailings and 80 tons of bullion, totalling 118,172 tons. For the same period, from Carson City back to Virginia City, freight carried consisted of 21,010 tons of merchandise, 35,457 tons of lumber, 54,210 tons of wood, 19,534 tons of coal and stone, and 110 tons of livestock for a total of 130,321 tons. Five years of booming business followed. Up to 50 trains operated over the single track line each day. Non-passenger trains outgoing from Virginia City carried ore for the mills totalling 80 to 100 carloads a day. Others returned from Carson City and Reno with wood and lumber (about 100 carloads a day in 1875) and other merchandise, hay, machinery, ice, etc. (20 to 40 carloads daily). Crews worked 18 hours a day, making four round trips.

During this boom time, 40 miles of spur tracks were built to various mines and mills. Another spur was extended from the main line to just above the mills at Silver City. In 1874, the main line rails between Carson City and Virginia City had to be replaced with new and heavier steel rails to carry the increased traffic. Capital stock of the V&T was increased to $5 million.

When Ormsby, Storey and Washoe counties attempted to tax the V&T, the V&T financial statements showed an amazing increase in the cost of construction and equipment. The assessed value was cut to $11,333 per mile and the V&T managed to pay little in taxes. The counties struggled for years with their bond issues.

In 1875 the Bank of California failed because of bad investments and William Sharon was worth some $70 million. Most of the banks's subsidiaries were lost and Ralston was forced out, his body found in San Francisco Bay shortly thereafter. The V&T was now owned one-third by Sharon and two-thirds by Mills. Also in 1875 the 55 mile V&T Railroad declared $360,000 in annual dividends and Darius Ogden Mills was elected president of the V&T. The following year the V&T surveyed a possible extension southward from Carson City to Genoa. The period from 1876 to 1878 was the most prosperous in the V&T's history, with 30 regularly scheduled trains and, at times, as many as 50 trains in service each day. In 1878, as quickly as it started, the boom ended.

THE DECLINING YEARS

In 1879, less than 20 percent of the ore tonnage hauled three years earlier was transported to the mills along the Carson River. Surplus locomotives were sold. With the decline of the V&T, Sharon and Mills looked for other railroads in which to invest. To help the struggling V&T Sharon and Mills decided to build the Carson & Colorado Railroad, a narrow gauge line beginning and connecting with the V&T at Mound House and continuing southward through Dayton, Hawthorne and over Montgomery Pass into the Owens Valley, 293 miles to Keeler at Owens Lake, California. Construction of the C&C started at Mound House in May 1880, reaching Keeler in 1881. The first three years of C&C operations were profitable, including interchange traffic with the V&T. After that, mining in the southern counties slumped and both railroads suffered economically. The line would never reach its intended end, the Colorado River.

Around 1886, the spur line to Silver City was abandoned. By 1888, freight hauled by the V&T to Virginia City had dropped off 86 percent. V&T dividends were eliminated in the 1890s. In 1900 the Southern Pacific bought the Carson & Colorado for $2,750,000 (renamed the Nevada & California Railway in 1905). Following an increase in taxes in 1901, many miles of V&T spur tracks were removed.

In 1901, talks began about extending the V&T from Carson City southward some 15 miles into the Carson Valley farming area, the Minden branch. By 1903, ore production improved in some of the mines and token dividend payments resumed. On November 17, 1903, a fire damaged the Homestead Tunnel, which took two months to repair.

Meanwhile, gold and silver was discovered at Tonopah in 1900 and at Goldfield in 1902. The Nevada and California Railroad was able to replace its narrow gauge rails to become standard gauge between Mound House and Tonopah Junction in 1905. When the V&T would not sell to the Southern Pacific, the Southern Pacific constructed the Hazen cutoff in 1905, bypassing the V&T altogether.

On June 24, 1905, the Virginia & Truckee Railway was formed to take over the Virginia & Truckee Railroad Co. for the purpose of constructing the Minden branch. Rail laying commenced in mid-April 1906, and train service began August 1, 1906. As Virginia City traffic became almost non-existent, the Minden run helped keep the railroad solvent.

In 1910, the V&T constructed a 2,000 foot spur to a new mill at Merrimac. In 1917, 90 of the eight ton ore cars were scrapped and in the early 1920s the last construction consisted of a 1.6 mile spur line to serve a mill at American Flat. Dividends continued to be paid until 1924.

After 1924, the V&T operated in the red. Ogden Mills acquired full control in 1933 and kept the line operating with his own personal funds until his death in 1937. Receivership followed in 1938. With dormant mines, the Virginia City to Carson City segment was abandoned and the rails were pulled in 1941, yielding $52,000 as scrap.

By 1949, the Reno to Carson City to Minden portion of the V&T could no longer economically continue. Locomotive inspection requirements could not be met and there was no money for repairs. Following extended hearings, abandonment was approved and the last train ran from Reno to Carson City on May 31, 1950, marking the end of the 81-year old V&T railroad.

The history of the V&T can boast a list of notables who rode the railroad that would include most of the names that made news in the United States during the last quarter of the Nineteenth Century. The V&T was there for the championship fight in Virginia City between Bob Fitzsimmons and Jim Corbett in March 1897. Many of the V&T coaches and older locomotives were sold to the movie companies of Hollywood and have been seen in movies such as "Union Pacific" and "The Great Locomotive Chase," or put on display.

The locomotives "Inyo," "Dayton" and "No. 25" can be viewed at the Nevada State Railroad Museum in Carson City.

In 1976, a short V&T railroad line was re-established in Virginia City for tourists that has now been extended to Gold Hill. Today, 1995, there is talk of extending the line to Carson City sometime in the near future.

VIRGINIA CITY, 1880, LOOKING EAST TO SUGAR LOAF MOUNTAIN.
Courtesy of Nevada Historical Society.

THE GREAT FIRE OF 1875

DURING THE 1860s AND 70s, many cities, towns and villages across the U.S. were fire traps. Wooden side-by-side construction, coupled with candles, oil lamps, lanterns, wood stoves, carelessness, lack of water and fire fighting equipment, and the wind made for devastating fires.

Virginia City was no exception. During the 20 year period from 1860 to 1880, Virginia City and Gold Hill suffered dozens of fires, wiping out entire residential areas and business blocks, only to be quickly rebuilt and await the next fire.

From 1861 to 1866, seven volunteer fire companies were formed in Virginia City and three in Gold Hill. The competition between the fire companies was fierce, sometimes resulting in fights and riots to determine which company would occupy the best position to fight a particular fire. There were two types of fires: the city fires of homes and businesses (the three largest occurring in 1863, 1871 and 1875 are shown on the map on pages 28-29); and the mine fires, the largest occurring in 1869 at the Crown Point and Yellow Jacket mines in Gold Hill with 45 lives lost.

The following article appeared in the October 27, 1875 issue of the *Virginia City Territorial Enterprise*, the day following the Great Fire of 1875.

YESTERDAY MORNING, at 5:30 o'clock, a fire broke out in a lodging-house on A Street, about midway between Taylor and Union streets, and nearly in the rear of William Mooney's livery stable, and soon got beyond the control of the Fire Department, when it swept through and destroyed nearly the whole of the business part of the city. Before water was got on the fire several wooden buildings adjoining the lodging-house were on fire, and it was plainly to be seen that a great fire was imminent. A heavy wind was blowing from the west, and this veered about in all directions as the fire increased in magnitude, firing

VIRGINIA CITY IN RUINS

—A Fearful and Uncontrollable Conflagration—

—The Heart of the City Swept Away —

—Several Thousand Persons Homeless—

—The Immediate Loss Probably About $7,000,000 —

—Consolidated Virginia Hoisting Works and the New California Stamp Mill Destroyed—

—But Little Property Saved Anywhere in the City.—

buildings on all sides with alarming rapidity. It was soon seen that the efforts of the firemen to control the flames would be fruitless, and the people began to exert themelves to save their goods. The wildest confusion prevailed, as all saw that, exert themselves as they might, the rapidly advancing flames must soon overwhelm their homes and household goods and gods.

Although the general course of the wind was from the west, yet the flames rapidly backed up against it and also moved at great speed to the north and south, while they rushed at race-horse speed to the eastward, making great leaps from building to building.

THE BURNED DISTRICT

When the fire was finally subdued, it had swept away all of that part of the city lying between Taylor street on the south, Carson street on the north, Stewart street on the west and the Chinese quarter on the east. The fire even exceeded these bounds, as on the south it crossed Taylor street on B and C streets and destroyed much valuable property; also crossed again below D street, when it destroyed the Catholic Church, the Methodist Church and many fine residences.

It also crossed Carson Steet and destroyed a considerable number of valuable buildings in that direction.

The fire everywhere made a clean sweep; none of the buildings supposed to be fire-proof stood the test. The flames passed through the majority of the brick buildings almost as rapidly as though they had been of wood. The firemen and the people were driven from point to point, and all appeared stupified and powerless, saying: "Nothing can be done. The fire must burn itself out." It was plainly to be seen that this was but too true. There was nothing to prevent the flames going as far as food for them was to be found.

A WILD SCENE

[A wild scene] was presented when the fire was at its he[i]ght. Viewed from the elevated ground to the westward the city was a sea of flames, from which vast columns of inky smoke rose hundreds of feet into the air. On all side[s] was heard the roar of the fire, the crash of falling roofs and walls, and every few minutes tremendous explosions of black and giant powder, as buildings were blown up in various parts of the town. Some of these explosions were so heavy that they are said to have rattled crockery and glassware in the town of Dayton, five miles distant. In all directions and all the streets the people were seen lugging along trunks, articles of furniture and bundles of bedding and clothing. No sooner had they deposited their loads in what was supposed to be a place of safety than the advancing flames compelled them to make another retreat. Many persons thus moved their goods from six to eight times, their pile growing less at each removal till at last they found themselves left with a mere handful of property.

Furniture of all kinds was consumed after it had been carried into the streets, and not a few pianos were thus abandoned to their fate after they had been carried out of buildings.

SOME OF THE PRINCIPAL BUILDINGS BURNED

At the present writing it is impossible to give even what would approach to a correct list of losses. We can only mention a few of the principal buildings, public and private, that have been burned: Between A and B street, beginning at the south, there was burned the residence of William Wood, the house of the

Eagle Engine Company, No. 3, Derby and Garhart's livery stable, Schleweck's lodging-house, Mrs. Cooper's buildings, the Noyes' building, Wilson & Brown's undertaking establishment, William Mooney's livery stable, Babcock's saloon, the Court-house, with County Jail and all of the county offices, the Washoe Club room, Virginia Hotel, Fulton Market, Filliott's grocery and provision store, Piper's saloon, Miner's Hall, Pioneer Hall, Capital lodging-house, residence of Thos. Buckner, and a great number of smaller buildings of all kinds. To the northward of Sutton Avenue was destroyed the large new residence of Judge B.C. Whitman, and those of E. Strother, W.E.F. Deal, Fred. Boegle, with scores of other fine buildings of various kinds. In the western part of the town were destroyed the fine residences of John Mack[a]y, J.P. Martin, Charles Forman, Charles Rawson, Judge Seely, F.A. Tritle, Charles Tozer, R.M. Daggett, W.B. Crane, A. Aurich, P.F. Beardsley, A. Hauak, Harry Block, D.E. McCarthy, Judge Rising, Joseph Beers, Oscar Steele, P.H. Scott, Thomas Gracey, C.M. Mayer, Simon Schlwek, and so many others that we cannot undertake to make mention of them at this time. On the west side of C street a clean sweep was made, from and including Marye's large new brick building all the way out to Carson street. Here was destroyed Williams & Bixler's building, Mailon's store, Barnett's clothing store, the Bank of California, the clothing store of Banner Brothers, John Gillig's hardware store, M.M. Fredrick's jewelry store, Union Market, Philadelphia shoe store, A. Vaenberg's dry goods store, Roos Brothers' clothing store, Block & Co., dry goods; Fletcher & Co., furniture; Magnolia saloon, Cohn & Isaacs, clothing; Washington, Assembly and Delta saloons, Harris Brothers, cigars; International Hotel and saloon, Palace saloon, Gobey & Williams' saloon, Theordore Wolf's tailor shop, the old Masonic Block, Berck's dry goods store, City Bakery, Thiele's drug store, the grocery and provision store of McMillan & Adams, new Masonic Building, J. Cornwell, furniture; Magel, meat market; J.J. Cooper's stables, hay-yard and large lodging house; Dickman's grocery store, Dellepiane's restaurant, the City Hall and many other fine buildings. On the east side of C street, beginning at Taylor, was destroyed Black's large brick building, in which were many offices and businesses—among others the offices of the Virginia "Evening Chronicle" and the "Footlight"; the ENTERPRISE building and office, J.C. Currie's auction, Noe's photograph gallery, Cook & Schonfelt's furniture store, the grocery and provision store of Hatch Brothers, Central Market, Philadelphia Brewery, Carson Brewery, Washington Guard Hall, Postoffice and building, James Kelly's liquor store and soda factory, store of J.C. Hampton & Co., house of Knickebocker Engine Company No. 6, Conrad Wiegand's assay office, Mrs. Emory's lodging house, McCutchen and Kruttecnicht's lodging houses, Lackey & Smith's lumber yard, J.C. Smith's blacksmith shop and many other buildings.

In the eastern part of the city the more prominent buildings burned were the Catholic Church, a splendid brick structure; the Methodist Church, St. Paul's Episcopal Church, the residence of Bishop Whitaker and D. Driscoll, the well-known stock-broker, with all the blocks of buildings lying north of Taylor street and east of D as far north as to and some distance beyond Carson street, going east through Chinatown and nearly to the C and C shaft.

Piper's Opera House was blown up after it was in flames, yet made a great and intensely hot fire. The freight and passenger depots of the Virginia and Truckee Railroad Company were in flames soon after the fire attacked the Opera House, and from these buildings the fire soon reached the Consolidated Virginia hoisting works; thence traveled to and destroyed the big mill of the company named and the new stamp-mill of the California Company. Shortly

MAP of VIRGINIA CITY
SHOWING HISTORIC LANDMARKS
AND
EARLY FIRES

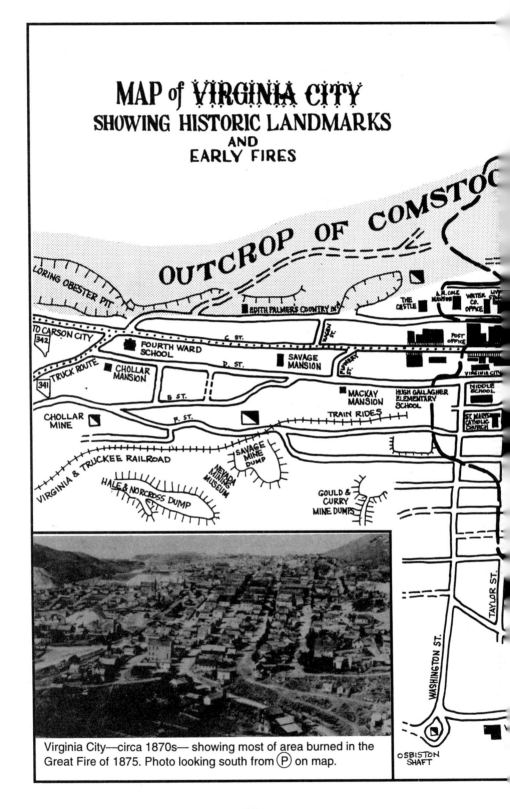

Virginia City—circa 1870s— showing most of area burned in the Great Fire of 1875. Photo looking south from (P) on map.

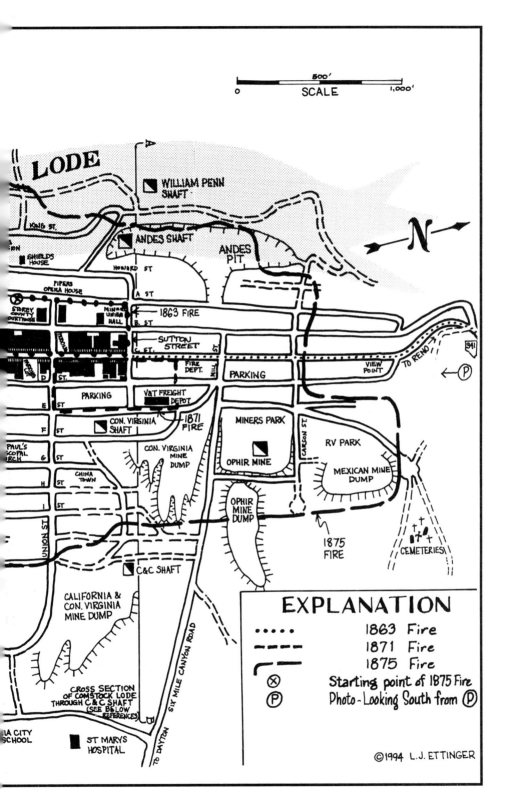

SCALE
500'
0   1,000'

LODE

WILLIAM PENN SHAFT

KING ST.

ANDES SHAFT

SHIELDS HOUSE

HOWARD ST

ANDES PIT

PIPERS OPERA HOUSE

A ST

STOREY COUNTY COURTHOUSE

MINERS UNION HALL

1863 FIRE

B. ST

SUTTON STREET

C. ST.

MILL ST

FIRE DEPT.

PARKING

VIEW POINT

TO RENO

341

D ST.

E ST

PARKING

V&T FREIGHT DEPOT

MINERS PARK

F ST

CON. VIRGINIA SHAFT

1871 FIRE

PAUL'S SCOPAL RCH

G ST

CON. VIRGINIA MINE DUMP

OPHIR MINE

CARSON ST

RV PARK

MEXICAN MINE DUMP

H ST

CHINA TOWN

I ST

OPHIR MINE DUMP

UNION ST

1875 FIRE

CEMETERIES

C&C SHAFT

CALIFORNIA & CON. VIRGINIA MINE DUMP

SIX MILE CANYON ROAD

TO DAYTON

CROSS SECTION OF COMSTOCK LODE THROUGH C & C SHAFT (SEE BELOW REFERENCES)

LA CITY SCHOOL

ST MARYS HOSPITAL

EXPLANATION

.....   1863   Fire
- - - -   1871   Fire
⌐ ─   1875   Fire
⊗   Starting point of 1875 Fire
Ⓟ   Photo - Looking South from Ⓟ

©1994 L.J. ETTINGER

after the Ophir works were on fire, and soon all in that neighborhood was a sea of flames. At the Consolidated Virginia and Ophir mines immense quantities of timbers, wood and lumber were destroyed, burning fiercely and for a great length of time.

THE MINES

As the fire approached the hoisting works of the several mines, the men were brought up from the lower levels, and all were safe on the surface before the flames reached the buildings surrounding the shafts. The top of the Consolidated Virginia shaft was bulkheaded and covered to a considerable depth with dirt, rendering it quite secure, as is supposed. At the Ophir shaft the cages were let down into their several compartments and the safety apparatus sprung when waste rock was shoveled in upon them. One of the cages gave way at the last moment and left its compartments open. It is thought that a portion of the timbers of the shaft were burned, as a strong smell of gas from burning pine came up the Gould and Curry shaft for a time yesterday afternoon. The hoisting compartments of the Curry were then closed, and the column of the pump opened so that the water, after being brought to near the surface, was allowed to fall back, thus driving the air and gases back whence they came. Even though the timbers in the Ophir should take fire it would be impossible for the flames to extend into the California, as between the two mines there is a space of about 300 feet in which there are no timbers. The burning of the hoisting works and mills will throw a small army of men out of employment, and men, too, in many instances, who have lost their homes and all they contained. These people, and hundreds of others, will need immediate assistance from abroad.

ACCIDENTS AND INCIDENTS

Two men are known to have been killed during the fire, and many were badly hurt, while scores made hair-breadth escapes of all kinds. A Mr. Ketton, of Gold Hill, was killed while passing from C to D street by the falling of the wall of the Carson Brewery. Two or three men were pretty seriously injured by the same wall.

A man, who appeared to be considerably intoxicated, was killed in the Black building. He was in Ash's book and toy store and was throwing out toys to persons in front, the upper floors of the building being about to fall in at the time. He was urged to leave the building, but continued to joke and fling out toys. Suddenly something from above fell upon him and knocked him senseless to the floor. An attempt was made to get the man out, but it was unsuccessful, and he was left to his fate in the burning building.

Several narrowly escaped being crushed by falling walls, and several came near being hurt by the blowing up of buildings. A number of persons came near being burned in their rooms, and a few were rescued from third-story windows, some throwing themselves down upon mattresses placed for their reception. Several horses were burned alive, and cats were to be seen darting out of buildings with their tails on fire.

Two engines, the [B]abcock of Eagle Engine Company No. 3, and the Knickerbocker, No. 5—were lost by being cut off by the fire. A train of wood cars was caught at the north end of the track of the railroad, north of the Ophir, and totally destroyed. At the time the County buildings took fire, the Sheriff took the prisoners from the County jail and lodged them in the station-house; soon the station-house which is in the basement of the Opera House, was threatened and the prisoners were again removed; and, to make sure of their safety, they were this time taken out to Cedar Hill and shut up in the old Sierra Nevada tunnel.

There was much stealing during the fire, and in some instances men were obliged to draw pistols in order to prevent their property being carried off by thieves. Last night the several military companies were ordered out, and were on duty in various parts of the town. A regular old-fashioned Washoe Zephyr set in soon after dark, walls were blown down in all directions, and suffocating clouds of dust and ashes were whirled through the burnt district, rendering duty in the streets exceedingly disagreeable.

The Post Office will be reopened in the Beardsley building, South C street. The Western Union Telegraph Company, who were burned out by the fire which a short time since destroyed Odd Fellows' Hall, were again burned out yesterday at the store of J. and J.B. Mallon when they went out into the northern suburbs of the town running a pony into the city with dispatches.

ORIGIN OF THE FIRE

The lodging house in which the fire originated was kept by a woman named Kate Shea, sometimes called "Crazy Kate." A lodger who was almost suffocated in his room states that the fire started in the hall of the basement of the building, near a water closet. He says that all the fire he saw as he escaped from his room was at the point mentioned. The occupants of the house were generally a rowdy set of men and women, and it is said that some kind of drunken carouse was going on among them until about 2 o'clock yesterday morning. The house had been complained of as disorderly and a nuisance, and it was a great mistake that it was not closed at that time.

LOSSES AND INSURANCE

At this time it is almost impossible to estimate the total loss by the fire, but it is placed at from seven to ten millions of dollars. Many of the business houses destroyed had on hand immense stocks of goods, and the mills and hoist works cost about $300,000 each. Little could yesterday be ascertained in regard to insurance. None of the property destroyed was very heavily insured, however,

The firemen labored faithfully from first to last, and by night were well nigh exhausted. The Gold Hill firemen came up to the city and did good work, until the boiler of their steamer exploded.

◆

GOULD & CURRY SILVER MINE REDUCTION WORKS, 1861.
Courtesy of Nevada Historical Society.

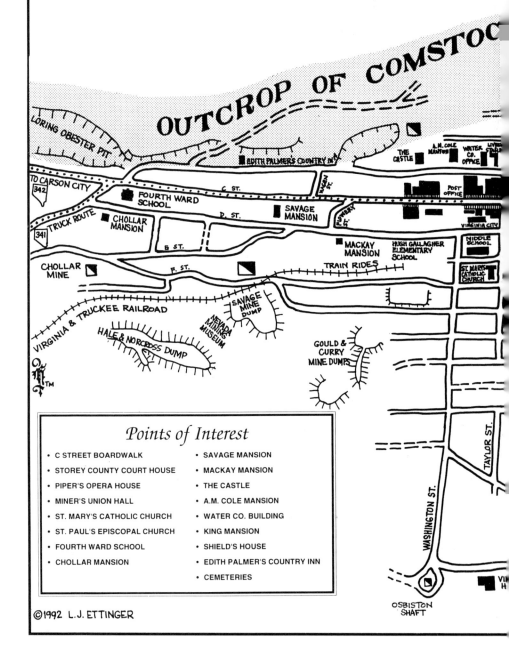

TOUR MAP of VIRGINIA CITY
SHOWING HISTORIC LANDMARKS

OUTCROP OF COMSTOC

LORING OBESTER PIT

TO CARSON CITY 342

TRUCK ROUTE 341

C. ST.

D. ST.

B ST.

E. ST.

FOURTH WARD SCHOOL

CHOLLAR MANSION

CHOLLAR MINE

EDITH PALMERS COUNTRY INN

NAGAN ST.

SAVAGE MANSION

FLOWERY ST.

MACKAY MANSION

THE CASTLE

A.M. COLE MANSION

WATER CO. OFFICE

LIVING STABLE

POST OFFICE

VIRGINIA CITY

HUGH GALLAGHER ELEMENTARY SCHOOL

MIDDLE SCHOOL

ST. MARYS CATHOLIC CHURCH

TRAIN RIDES

VIRGINIA & TRUCKEE RAILROAD

HALE & NORCROSS DUMP

NEVADA MINING MUSEUM

SAVAGE MINE DUMP

GOULD & CURRY MINE DUMPS

TM

WASHINGTON ST.

TAYLOR ST.

OSBISTON SHAFT

VI H

Points of Interest

- C STREET BOARDWALK
- STOREY COUNTY COURT HOUSE
- PIPER'S OPERA HOUSE
- MINER'S UNION HALL
- ST. MARY'S CATHOLIC CHURCH
- ST. PAUL'S EPISCOPAL CHURCH
- FOURTH WARD SCHOOL
- CHOLLAR MANSION

- SAVAGE MANSION
- MACKAY MANSION
- THE CASTLE
- A.M. COLE MANSION
- WATER CO. BUILDING
- KING MANSION
- SHIELD'S HOUSE
- EDITH PALMER'S COUNTRY INN
- CEMETERIES

©1992 L.J. ETTINGER

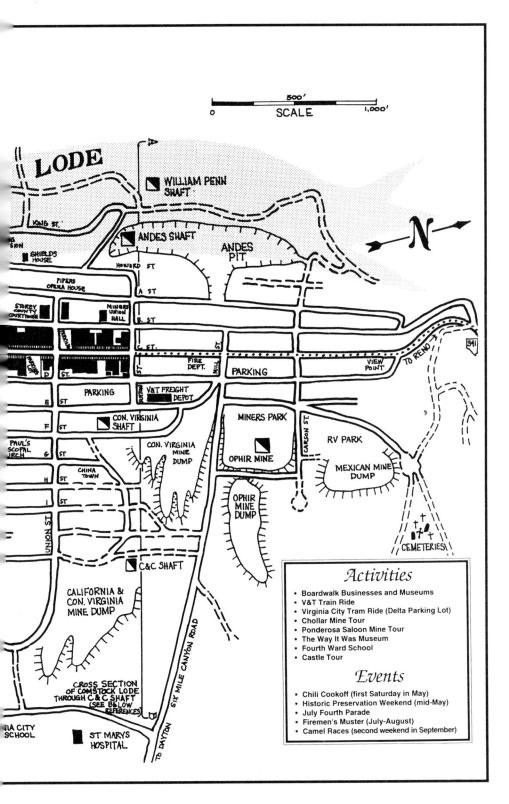

SCALE

500' · 1,000'

0

LODE

WILLIAM PENN SHAFT

KING ST.

ANDES SHAFT

ANDES PIT

SHIELDS HOUSE

HOWARD ST

PIPERS OPERA HOUSE

A ST

STOREY COUNTY COURTHOUSE

MINERS UNION HALL

B ST

C ST

FIRE DEPT.

PARKING

VIEW POINT

TO RENO

341

N

PARKING

E ST

V&T FREIGHT DEPOT

CON. VIRGINIA SHAFT

F ST

MINERS PARK

RV PARK

CARSON ST.

PAUL'S SCOPAL URCH

G ST

CON. VIRGINIA MINE DUMP

OPHIR MINE

MEXICAN MINE DUMP

CHINA TOWN

H ST

I ST

OPHIR MINE DUMP

UNION ST

CEMETERIES

C&C SHAFT

CALIFORNIA & CON. VIRGINIA MINE DUMP

SIX MILE CANYON ROAD

CROSS SECTION OF COMSTOCK LODE THROUGH C & C SHAFT (SEE BELOW REFERENCES)

TO DAYTON

IA CITY SCHOOL

ST MARYS HOSPITAL

Activities

- Boardwalk Businesses and Museums
- V&T Train Ride
- Virginia City Tram Ride (Delta Parking Lot)
- Chollar Mine Tour
- Ponderosa Saloon Mine Tour
- The Way It Was Museum
- Fourth Ward School
- Castle Tour

Events

- Chili Cookoff (first Saturday in May)
- Historic Preservation Weekend (mid-May)
- July Fourth Parade
- Firemen's Muster (July-August)
- Camel Races (second weekend in September)

THE SUTRO TUNNEL

ONE OF THE MOST EXCITING engineering projects to be undertaken on the Comstock, the Sutro Tunnel was conceived and promoted by one of the Comstock's most colorful personalities, Adolph Heinrich Sutro. An extremely intelligent achiever, an excellent communicator, both as a speaker and as a writer, Sutro fought for what he believed.

Born the third of 11 children in Aachem, Prussia, April 29, 1830, Sutro, as a boy growing up in Germany, was an avid reader. He was interested in the sciences, and attended school until he was 16. His family was well-to-do; his father owned a woolen cloth factory where Sutro learned mechanical skills. His father died when he was 18. This, coupled with numerous revolutions and rebellions sweeping Europe, led to the closure of the factory and the Sutro family immigrating to America. Sutro arrived in New York with his family when he was 20.

Two weeks later he sailed for San Francisco, crossed the Isthmus of Panama on foot, and arrived on November 21, 1850. Believing he could be more successful as a merchant than as a miner, within four years he owned several stores that specialized in imported tobaccos. He was also a wholesale supplier to stores in mining towns along the California Mother Lode. San Francisco was the starting-off place to the gold camps in California, the Oregon Territory and the Utah Territory, and Sutro, like many of that time, had "gold fever."

When the gold rush to the Mother Lode was over, Sutro looked elsewhere. He first saw the Comstock in its infancy in 1860, still as a part of Utah Territory. Sutro believed that he could invent a better way to treat the gold-silver rich quartz ores, and upon his return to San Francisco, he published a communication in the April 20, 1860 issue of the *Alta California* advocating a tunnel from near Dayton westward to cut the Comstock Lode at depth. He returned to the Comstock in 1862 and within a year built a steam-powered reducing mill along the Carson River at Dayton using the "Sutro Process," with eight stamps and 20 amalgamating pans.

EARLY MINING DEVELOPMENT

Meanwhile, the Comstock Lode, discovered in 1859, was thought to be a westward dipping quartz vein system striking north-south over a distance of some four miles. During the first two years the veins were mined from the surface adits and shafts (first-line, west of A Street) by primitive methods to depths of about 400 feet. Some water was encountered and drained through the adits or hauled to the surface in buckets by means first of a hand-powered windlass, and later by a horse and whim (drum).

In order to drain some of the properties served by the shafts, in 1861 the Latrobe Tunnel and Mining Company, under contract with several mining companies that would become the Consolidated Virginia Mine, drove a drainage and exploration tunnel (the Mint Tunnel). The tunnel portal was about one half mile east of Virginia City and was engineered to intersect the Comstock

Lode at a horizontal distance of 3,000 feet and at a depth of 600 feet below the outcroppings. The tunnel intersected the barren and broken Lode in 1864 at 2,800 feet, at about 700 feet on its dip. Drifts were then run to drain the nearby Central and Ophir mines.

In 1862 the Cedar Hill Tunnel and Mining Company began a drainage tunnel on the north end of the Lode, but gave up the project after 2,000 feet. In 1863, the Gold Hill and Virginia Tunnel and Mining Company disclosed plans to drive a drainage-exploration tunnel (the Daney Tunnel) the entire length of the Comstock Lode from a point in Gold Canyon near Silver City northward to a point 1,000 feet below the Ophir Mine at the north end of Virginia City, a horizontal distance of 15,000 feet. The tunnel was in progress for about a year when financing dried up because all the upper ore bodies on the Lode were mined out and no new ore bodies had been discovered at depth. The tunnel was never resumed.

The year 1863 was a boom year. The westward dipping veins and upper ore bodies were explored and mined to depths of about 500 feet where they intersected the main Comstock Fault and vein which dipped eastward at about 45 degrees. With this new information, during 1864 the second line shafts along D street were sunk to intersect the Comstock Fault and Lode at vertical depths of 600 feet, east of the outcrops. As shafts deepened, a large bucket was fastened to the bottom of an ore bucket which, when lowered by steam engine power, filled with water collected in a sump at the bottom of the shaft. Plunger pumps were also used.

THE SUTRO TUNNEL

The idea of a long tunnel from near the Carson River to the Comstock Lode at depth was discussed and the subject of editorial commentary during the early years of the Comstock.

The overall mining picture on the Comstock in 1863 can be summarized as follows. Most of the reduction mills were built along the Carson River. Ore and freight were hauled by wagon and teamster expenses were high. There was talk of building a railroad from Virginia City to the mills and then to Carson City, but with little action. The deepening mines were encountering hot water and ventilation was also a problem.

Sutro's mill burned in late 1863. It appears to have been a profitable operation and was insured for a large sum. With no mill and with the "tunnel" in the back of his mind for several years, Sutro was able to turn his attention to a tunnel project. He was well aware of the widespread interest in a drainage tunnel which could also be used as an inexpensive means of transporting ore to the Carson River for reduction where water was available for power and also for bringing in the great quantity of timber used in the mines. The mining companies had encouraged the past drainage tunnel projects and they encouraged Sutro, especially when he proposed to raise the money for the work abroad.

Sutro was intelligent enough to know of the power that went to whoever built and owned the "tunnel." That person could control draining and ventilation of the mines, transport and milling of ore, and shipment of freight. The "tunnel" idea was gaining momentum as shown in a March 14, 1864, *Gold Hills News* editorial on "the necessity for a tunnel five or six miles in length to drain the mines."

Sutro "sighted" a tunnel location that would start at a point between Corral and Webber canyons three miles north of Dayton and run west-north-west to a point under Mount Davidson.

SUTRO THE PROMOTER

In late 1864, Sutro petitiond the Nevada State Legislature and on February 4, 1865, an Act was passed granting to "A. Sutro and his associates an exclusive franchise to construct and operate a tunnel for a period of 50 years." He was required to begin construction within one year and complete the tunnel within eight years.

Sutro proceeded to have the land surveyed for his tunnel and began to put together a prospectus. On July 24, 1865, the Sutro Tunnel Company was organized. William M. Stewart, a Comstock lawyer and U.S. Senator from the new state of Nevada, was named as company president.

The new Sutro Tunnel Company now had two priority goals: to obtain contracts with the mining companies to be served by the tunnel and to raise funding to build the tunnel. During the remainder of 1865, Sutro and his attorneys negotiated with the mining companies and their attorneys, coming to agreements whereby the Sutro Tunnel Company would be paid a royalty of two dollars for every ton of ore extracted after the Sutro Tunnel reached each mine. This fee was for drainage and ventilation only. Additional fees of 25 cents per mile per ton were for removal of ore through the tunnel or for haulage of wood or other materials from the mouth of the tunnel to the mines. Transport of men through the tunnel would cost 25 cents each. Contracts were signed in April 1866 by 23 of the principal mining companies representing 95 percent of the stock market value of the Comstock Lode.

Fundraising involved educating the public and Sutro did this by a number of published reports. He hired Baron Richthofen, a well-known geologist of the times, to prepare a full-length report on the Comstock Lode and the proposed Sutro Tunnel, which was published as an 83-page booklet in 1866.

The Richthofen Report concluded that the Comstock Lode was a "true fissure vein" that would continue in depth; that the $50 million already extracted in gold and silver was but a small proportion of the amount of gold and silver remaining to be extracted at lower levels. Richthofen also recommended the Sutro Tunnel to drain the mines at depth, provide ventilation and access, and explore the lower parts of the Comstock Lode.

Sutro knew that the land through which his tunnel would traverse was owned by the U.S. government and that he would need congressional consent to begin his project. Armed with the Richthofen Report, Sutro left San Francisco for Washington, D.C. on May 10, 1866, via Panama and the new Panama Railroad. He arrived in Washington in early June.

Using congressional influence, Senator Stewart introduced and Congress passed, the Sutro Tunnel Act which President Andrew Johnson signed on July 25, 1866. The Act granted the Sutro Mining Company the right-of-way for a tunnel and empowered Sutro to purchase 4,375 acres of land at the mouth of the tunnel for $1.25 an acre and any mineral lands (including mineral rights) within 2,000 feet on either side of the tunnel at $5.00 an acre, excepting the Comstock Lode and existing occupied mining claims. The Sutro Tunnel Act also provided that every mine that benefited from the tunnel must pay for that benefit, either negotiated or not. The Act had no forfeiture clause, or time limit on the life of the grant and no time limit set for completion of the tunnel. More important, this federal grant superseded the Nevada Act with its time limits because federal lands were involved. Sutro had covered all his bases.

Sutro went to New York in August 1866 to sell stock to build his tunnel. He had published a prospectus pamphlet which concluded that the $2 million cost to dig the tunnel would see an annual payback of between $2.3 and $6 million. Sutro also prophesized in his prospectus that the majority of the population of Virginia City and Gold Hill would shift to his new town of Sutro at the mouth of the tunnel, along with construction of new mills powered by water drained from the tunnel. East coast investors were interested and told Sutro that if he could raise about one half million dollars on the west coast that they would raise about $1 million on the east coast.

Sutro returned to the Comstock in late 1866 knowing that he had a time limit in his mining company royalty contracts; i.e., that he had to raise $3 million in stock subscriptions with at least 10 percent paid in cash by August 1, 1867, and that he had to start construction no later than that same date.

By May 1867, Sutro had stock subscriptions of $600,000 from 11 of the mining companies (which also granted a one year extension to commence operations) and individuals.

OTHER DEVELOPMENTS

While Sutro was getting his Sutro Tunnel Company moving, other events were happening that would greatly affect the tunnel, the time table of construction, and the ultimate fate of the project.

The Bank of California, controlled by William Ralston, was formed in San Francisco in 1864 and opened a Virginia City branch later that year. Managed by William Sharon, the branch provided loans to the Comstock mining companies at a lower interest rate than other banks. During hard times the bank foreclosed on a number of the mining companies and mills and transferred title to the Union Mill and Mining Company whose shareholders owned the Bank of California. By 1867, the Union Mill and Mining Company was a monopoly which had consolidated all the important independent operators on the Comstock and a number of mills along the Carson River. Ralston and Sharon dictated a great deal of what happened on the Comstock and initially they favored Sutro's tunnel project because it would benefit them financially.

CONFLICT

By early 1867, Ralston, Sharon and their associates learned of Sutro's "prophesy" and realized that Sutro was out to undermine their power base. Sutro underestimated their power and the battle was on. Sutro's early supporters abandonded him and sided with Sharon and the powerful Bank of California and its Union Mill and Mining Company. The $600,000 pledges for stock subscriptions would never be ratified and Sutro had to look to new money.

Sutro was, for all purposes, "persona non grata" on the Comstock and over the next two years he would spend much of his time on the road, traveling to New York, Washington, D.C. and Europe looking for funding, without success.

Sutro, for Congress and potential investors, wrote and published a book, "The Mineral Resources of the United States" in 1868, describing his tunnel and the benefits to be derived from it. Sharon and Ralston put their own pressure on Congress not to get involved in the Sutro Tunnel project. Sutro had two tunnel subsidy bills introduced in Congress but neither passed, largely due to Ralston and Sharon's congressional influence.

1865-1869

During the five-year period from 1865 through 1869 when Sutro began to promote his tunnel, the Comstock saw depression in 1865, followed by good years between 1866 and 1868 as new ore bodies were found, and then followed by another decline in 1869.

During this period about 1,500 miners were at work producing about 1,500 tons of ore per day from the few producing mines. Exploration was intense. A number of the second line shafts which intersected the main Comstock Lode at about 600 feet vertical depth were being deepened as inclines eastward along the Lode to depths of 800 to 900 feet. The Bullion Mine incline reached a depth of 1,400 feet in barren rock. The deeper the mines got, the hotter the ground and the greater the water problem. Root blowers were introduced in 1865 and helped somewhat with the ventilation problems.

As early as 1866 due to the high cost of wagon teamsters hauling ore to the mills and freight back to the mines at Virginia City, Sharon began thinking about building a railroad from Virginia City to Carson City and then to connect with the future Central Pacific Railroad along the Truckee River (at a place which would later become Reno).

Once Ralston and Sharon learned of Sutro's plans to "take over" the Comstock, they actively pursued the V&T Railroad project (see The V&T Railroad), as part of their effort to destroy Sutro and the tunnel project.

The V&T Railroad was in operation in early 1870, insuring the continued existence of Sharon's Comstock mills along the Carson River and greatly reducing freight costs (which also marked the end of the teamster business). The railroad also ended Sutro's claim of tunnel profits from hauling freight and as a faster route for man to travel.

THE TURNING POINT

On April 7, 1869, 45 men died in the great Yellow Jacket mine fire, which also engulfed the adjoining Crown Point and Kentuck mines. Most of the men died from asphyxiation because they were unable to escape the mines. Sharon and Ralston were accused of being negligent of the miner's welfare—it was claimed that Sutro's tunnel could have provided an escape route.

Sutro turned to the miners for support and got it. Using the argument that his tunnel would provide better underground working conditions by removing the hot water and providing natural ventilation, along with the safety of an additional escape route in case of fire, Sutro again approached the local newspapers and Congress. By mid-1869, the Miner's Union pledged $50,000 to the purchase of Sutro Tunnel stock.

On September 20, 1869, Sutro spoke to the miner's at Piper's Opera House. He gave a rousing speech that would increase support for his tunnel venture from the miner's, their union, and some of the local newspapers.

DIGGING THE TUNNEL

Finally, Sutro acquired enough money from stock subscriptions and on October 19, 1869, the tunnel ground breaking took place before 200 guests.

John Bethel was in charge of the tunnel construction and, with his crew of nine men using only hand tools, laid 52-1/2 feet of track the first 10 days. By November 26th they had penetrated 254 feet.

A new Sutro Tunnel Company was filed as a California Corporation on November 29th, with a total of 1,200,000, $10 par value, non-assessable shares of stock. Sutro turned over his Nevada and U.S. government tunnel franchise to the new corporation for 503,916 shares, an approximate 5/12 interest in the

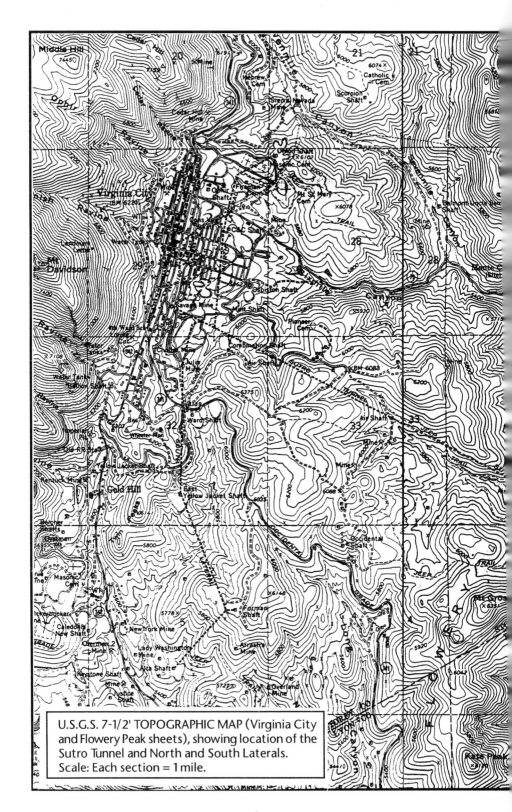

U.S.G.S. 7-1/2' TOPOGRAPHIC MAP (Virginia City and Flowery Peak sheets), showing location of the Sutro Tunnel and North and South Laterals.
Scale: Each section = 1 mile.

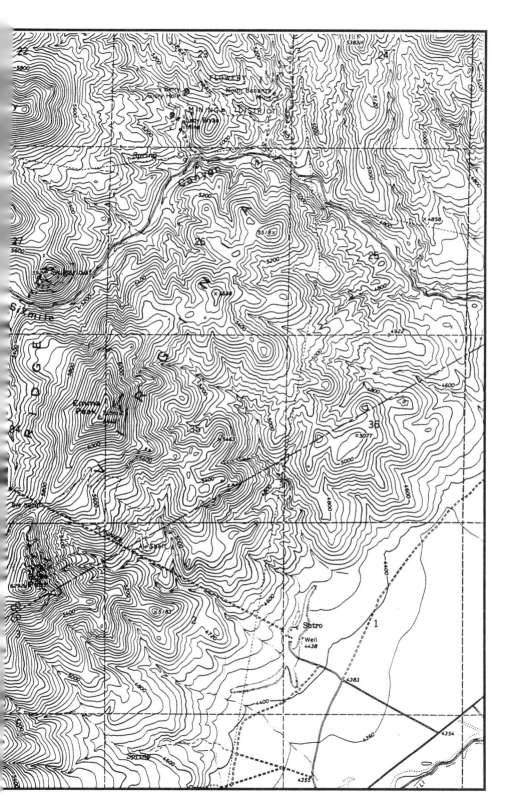

corporation, and was named General Superintendent of the Sutro Tunnel Project. Available to the public were 400,000 $10 par value shares.

In early 1870 Sutro returned to Washington, riding the new transcontinental railroad. He was, unsuccessfully, seeking government loans for his tunnel. With bills coming in he then sailed to London, again without success.

By September 1870, the three shifts of miners had been reduced to one, and Sutro was in San Francisco looking for financing. In December Sutro moved to Washington and lobbied Congress for a Sutro Tunnel Commission, which President Grant created on April 4, 1871. Meanwhile, one group of international bankers, the Seligmans, began advancing Sutro enough money to keep him afloat until he could get backing for the tunnel.

The federal tunnel commissioners were on site in Virginia City during the summer of 1871. They were being hosted by the mine owners and superintendents who were against the tunnel project. Other interested parties arrived at the same time and, through their own observations and the recommendations of others favorable to the project, advised financiers in London of the merits of the project.

In the fall of 1871, $650,000 in stock purchases was made (using gold coin) by Robert McCalmont. Sutro bought mining machinery and by December the tunnel project, with over 300 men employed, was moving ahead.

In December 1871, four shafts were started along the tunnel line for the purpose of providing eight additional surfaces for tunneling as well as for ventilation: Shaft No. 1—4,915 feet from the portal, projected 522 feet deep; Shaft No. 2—9,065 feet from the portal, projected 1,041 feet deep; Shaft No. 3—13,555 from the portal, projected 1,361 feet deep; and Shaft No. 4—17,695 feet from the portal, projected approximately 1,500 feet deep. Boarding houses were built at each shaft. The drop in elevation from Virginia City to the tunnel portal was about 1,600 feet, but was not a steady decline. The tunnel line went up and down six hills, making for a rough trip. Sutro had a wagon road built from the tunnel portal to Shaft No. 2 and then repaired an old road to Virginia City.

In early 1872, the tunnel was in 2,792 feet. Rock was removed by mule-pulled cars. No ore bearing veins were crossed.

The report of the Sutro Tunnel Commission was finished in early 1872, concluding that the Sutro Tunnel was "not a necessity." However, Congressional hearings which followed overruled the conclusions of the special commission and drew up a bill calling for a $2 million loan to the Sutro Tunnel Company, which was subsequently voted down.

Sutro would write and publish two books for promotional purposes titled, "Sutro Tunnel—1872" and "Mineral Resources of the United States."

Money was coming in monthly from the McCalmont Brothers in England and Sutro purchased diamond drills, "T" racks and steam pumps.

Sutro also purchased his townsite near the tunnel portal, had it surveyed and published a promotional map. On September 9, 1872, the first two lots were sold. Sutro was also constructing his mansion which was owned by the tunnel company and cost $40,000 to build and furnish. He also decided to be a candidate for the U.S. Senate, running as an independent against Sharon.

The tunnel company purchased two ranches, thereby obtaining three miles of Carson River frontage with stamp mill potential, and with hay fields and hay inventory used to feed the mules.

In 1873 work continued on the tunnel, cutting back when money was short. Sutro continued traveling between the Comstock, Washington, and Europe in his efforts to raise more money. Most of his success came from large stock purchases by Robert McCalmont.

Shaft No. 1 reached the tunnel level in mid-1873 and drifts were started in both directions to connect with the main tunnel and to continue to the east. Water was encountered in Shaft No 2, requiring pumps. Construction went ahead through 1873.

In early 1874, Ralston, Sharon and their group, called the "bank ring," stepped up their attack on the tunnel project, both in Congress and locally. Sharon bought the *Virginia City Enterprise* to go along with the *Virginia Chronicle* and the *Gold Hill News*.

On April 25, 1874, Burleigh compressed air drills were first used in the Sutro Tunnel, with operators hired after the five mile long Hoosac Railroad Tunnel in Masschusetts was finished.

In November 1874, Sharon easily won the election, becoming U.S. Senator from Nevada; however, Sharon did not take his seat in the Senate the first year and was absent the last four years of his six-year term.

Now, some five years after the tunnel started, it was in 8,079 feet. Sutro was again in London where the McCalmont Brothers told him that they would no longer buy stock (they now owned nearly half the tunnel stock) but instead would loan him the necessary money to keep going, with a first mortgage on all property of the tunnel company.

1870-1875

During the five year period 1870-1875, the Comstock was extremely active. The 1869 period of decline continued into 1870. A number of new ore bodies, including the Crown Point Bonanza, were discovered below 1,000 feet in 1871, leading to a revival on the Comstock and a boom year in 1872.

In 1871, the "Silver Kings" (The Firm), John W. Mackay, James C. Flood, James G. Fair and William S. O'Brien, began buying stock when prices were low, leading to controlling interest in the Con Virginia and California.

In 1873, exploration was going deeper along the Lode, the deepened second line shafts and inclines hitting hot water and hot rocks. The first of the great third-line shafts, the C&C, was started and the first of the giant Cornish pumps was installed. The year 1873 would be a boom year with the discovery of the Big Bonanza ore body in March, allowing the "Silver Kings" to challenge the power of Sharon and Ralston. The richness of the bonanza carried through 1874 with a wild stock market, stocks increasing in value throughout the year and would crash in early 1875.

By 1875 the "Big Bonanza" had brought enough wealth to the "Silver Kings" that they were entirely independent of Ralston and Sharon. After the high stock prices of January, the market became erratic, causing problems with the Bank of California. Panic swept San Francisco and on August 26th the Bank of California was besieged with depositors and had to close. The following day Ralston's body washed up on the bay shores. The "Bank Crowd" would be no more.

On October 26, 1875, most of Virginia City burned to the ground with a property loss of some $10 million. By the end of the year 1875 the tunnel had advanced 3,726 feet.

WORK ON THE TUNNEL CONTINUES

The tunnel excavation continued throughout 1876.

The stock market revived as the Comstock had one of its best years. Third-line vertical shafts were being sunk east of Virginia City to intersect the lode at depths between 2,500 to 4,500 feet.

GOLD HILL

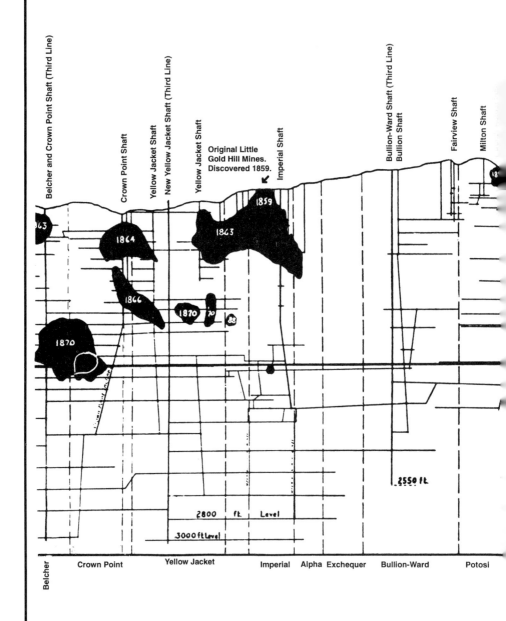

VIRGINIA CITY

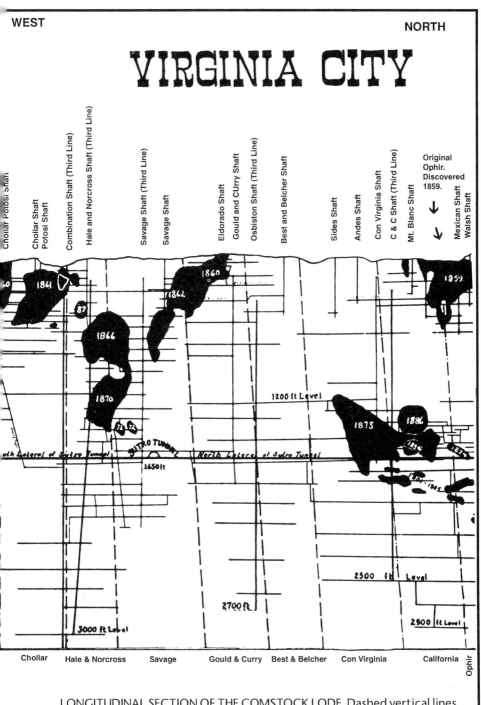

LONGITUDINAL SECTION OF THE COMSTOCK LODE. Dashed vertical lines are mining claim boundaries. Solid lines are mine workings. Black areas are orebodies with dates of their discovery. The "Big Bonanza" orebody (1873) is seen between the 1,200 and 1,650 foot levels north of the Sutro Tunnel.

By 1877 the great bonanza ore body terminated at the 1,650 foot level, ending the bonanza period. It was the start of the decline of the Comstock and the Sutro Tunnel was not yet completed.

In early 1878, the project boss described the heat encountered as "being sufficient to cook a chicken in half an hour." There were 102 mules and almost 1,000 men working underground.

By April, Sutro was well aware that the mine owners still did not back his tunnel and he also knew that his royalty agreement was not enforceable because the time requirements had not been met. Sutro ordered the erection of a bulkhead that could be used to seal the tunnel if royalties could not be collected from the mine owners. There were many problems with bad ground, the heat and ventilation. The mules used to haul the waste cars were dropping dead.

THE TUNNEL IS COMPLETED

In early July, the tunnel was close to breaking through and on July 8, 1878, the tunnel made contact with an east drift on the 1,640 level of the Savage Mine incline. That day and the next was for celebration. It took eight years, eight months, and 19 days to complete the 20,498 foot tunnel.

Before Sutro would allow the tunnel to be used for drainage, he needed a new royalty agreement with the mining companies who now refused to pay a royalty of $2/ton. A drainage ditch needed to be constructed in the tunnel, and north and south laterals needed to be excavated joining the various mines with the main tunnel.

In January 1879, some of the main mines were having serious water problems and wanted to connect with the Sutro Tunnel. Sutro was attempting to re-negotiate an agreement and both the mine owners and Sutro were threatening each other. The mine owners were threatening to release hot water into the tunnel without the ditch being completed, and Sutro threatened to close his bulkhead.

On February 16, two of the mines started their pumps flushing water into the Sutro Tunnel and men and mules had to run for their lives. The pumping continued for two days.

Finally, on April 2, a new agreement was signed by 24 mining companies, whereby the tunnel company agreed to have the drainage ditch in the tunnel completed in 90 days, and the mining companies agreed to pay a royalty of $1.00 for every ton of ore with a mill head of under $40, and $2.00 for every ton of ore with a mill head greater than $40. The mines agreed to advance $70 per running foot of laterals driven north and south to their mines.

On June 30, 1879, the first line of 3'x3' drainage boxes were ready to receive water and a second drainage ditch was half completed. The first water, measured at 104-1/2°F., came through the open ditch at the mouth of the tunnel with a great cloud of steam.

In 1880 Sutro, foreseeing the decline of the Comstock, resigned his position as superintendent of the Sutro Tunnel Company, and moved to San Francisco selling his company stock for $709,012. He invested in San Francisco real estate, was elected Mayor of San Francisco in 1894, and died there in 1898.

With new agreements with the mine owners, the north and south laterals were started and completed by 1884.

The north lateral, 4,403 feet in length, reached the Union Shaft on October 4, 1880, and drained 3.5 million gallons of hot water daily. By March 1, 1881 the South Lateral reached the Yellow Jacket Shaft at 4,114 feet and extended to the Alta Shaft, a distance of 8,433 feet, by 1888. After completion of the laterals between 3.5 to 4 million gallons of hot water flowed through the Sutro Tunnel daily (1.2 billion gallons yearly).

THE TUNNEL AFTER COMPLETION
During the first five years after completion of the tunnel annual revenues from royalties and transport charges averaged $44,000, then increased to about $100,000 per year during the low-grade mining period (1884-1895). The tunnel was a financial burden for five or six years after its completion because the Sutro Tunnel Company stock was non-assessable. The McCalmonts fought to foreclose their mortgages for the $1,575,225 owing. No part of the cost of the tunnel was ever repaid except for $800,000 paid to the McCalmonts as a negotiated settlement when the property of the Sutro Tunnel Company was sold in foreclosure in 1889. A new company, the Comstock Tunnel Company, took over the property.

The Sutro Tunnel, however, was about 10 years too late. Had it been completed in the early 1870s, it would have saved the mining companies millions of dollars in pumping costs. As it was, several of the shafts were 500 feet deeper than the 1,640 tunnel level when it reached the Lode and no deep ore was discovered, nor was any ore discovered because of the tunnel nor did the air serve as a satisfactory means of ventilation after passing through the hot, wet tunnel.

During the 50 years following completion of the tunnel and its laterals, the Gold Hill mines, with hot waters of 150°F, were automatically drained through the tunnel. In the Virginia City mines, the water stood about 100 feet below the tunnel level after 1884, except for a brief period after 1900 when the north end mines were pumped out to the 2,500 foot level.

In the early 1900s, a new steam-tight stovepipe drain was installed in the tunnel which cooled the entire tunnel. A new track was laid the length of the tunnel and the Savage Mining Company was operating the Comstock Tunnel Company mill at the mouth of the tunnel. Citizens of Dayton and Sutro would use the tunnel, riding up the C&C shaft to Saturday night dances in Virginia City. The mill was operated sporatically into the 1930s.

The townsite of Sutro never developed as Sutro dreamed it would. The mansion burned in the 1940s and the mill was destroyed by fire in 1967. Today, trees and brush almost obscure the portal and, behind the concrete facade, the tunnel is caved in for about 50 feet. Only a small stream of water flows out of the tunnel now. Waters from the mines are, for the most part, dammed off by cave-ins deep within the tunnel.

The Comstock Tunnel and Drainage Company still exists as does the Sutro Tunnel Company, which still owns property adjacent to the portal and the easement for the tunnel granted by Congress in 1866.

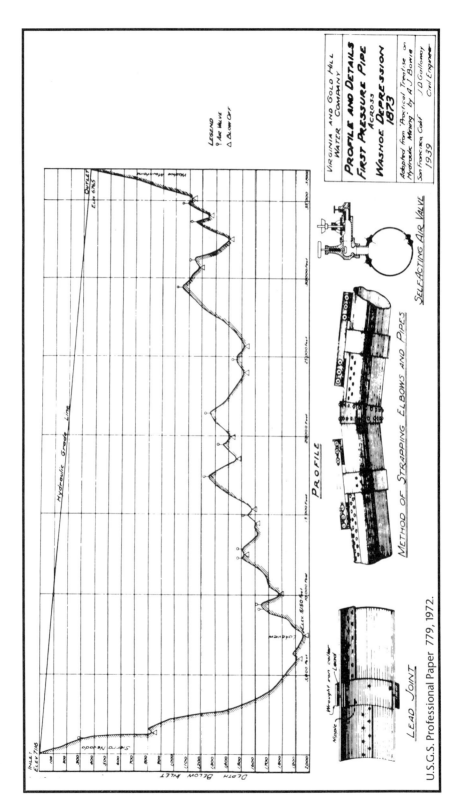

U.S.G.S. Professional Paper 779, 1972.

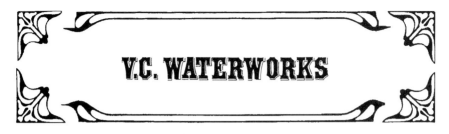

V.C. WATERWORKS

AN ENGINEERING AND CONSTRUCTION MARVEL of its time, the Comstock water works could not have been completed without the real and potential value of the silver and gold of the district. The Comstock, on the upper eastern side of the Virginia Range of mountains at an elevation of 6,200 feet, is within the upper desert environment of the Basin and Range Province. Precipitation is about eight inches a year with little surface runoff except in the winter and spring. Hot water (up to 170°F) with mineral salts was encountered as the miners dug deeper into the Comstock Fault.

THE EARLY DAYS

The first prospectors and miners in 1859 obtained their water from a few nearby springs in Ophir, Bullion and Crown Point Ravines, and then from adits as they were driven on the eastern slope of Mt. Davidson (Sun Mountain). In 1860 and 1861 the population of the camps of Virginia City and Gold Hill increased to boom town size. Water became scarce and, as it was brought into the area on the backs of mules, very expensive. One individual, Ned Foster, developed springs and sold water by the gallon or barrel, and in the winter packed thousands of sacks with snow, which he stored in the mine tunnels, selling them in the summer.

Two water companies, the Virginia Water Company and the Gold Hill Water Company, were formed. Water flowing from several adits dug into Mt. Davidson west of Virginia City and Gold Hill was collected in wooden tanks and piped into the two towns.

As the mines deepened and new ore was discovered in 1861, many mills were built at the mines, down Six Mile and Gold canyons, along the Carson River and in Washoe Valley to treat the silver-gold ore. All of these mills needed water to operate and those near Virginia City and Gold Hill competed for the scarce water supply.

Virginia City incorporated in 1861, with a population of about 4,000 which grew to 15,000 by the summer of 1862 (including Gold Hill). On May 12, 1862, the two water companies consolidated forming the Virginia and Gold Hill Water Company with a capital stock of $250,000.

THE VIRGINIA AND GOLD HILL WATER COMPANY

The new water company's main source of water was bought or leased from the owners of seven mines where water was flowing from the tunnels. The water was collected into large cisterns from flumes and ditches and distributed to Virginia City and Gold Hill. The first mains were wooden boxes, placed on or near the surface, with branch pipes of lead tubing. In August 1863, iron supply pipes were laid in South C Street.

In October 1863, Virginia City was receiving 664 gallons per minute (some 900,000 gallons per day), over 500 gallons of it coming from the Santa Rita Tunnel in Ophir Ravine. Each year, as Virginia City grew, the peril of water drought increased. Flumes and pipes which ran full in the Spring were half empty in Autumn. Water pumped from the mines was always charged with mineral salts. It was not potable and could not be used in the boilers.

In 1867, a prospecting adit, the Cole Tunnel, was driven into Ophir Ravine below the Santa Rita Tunnel and hit a broken quartz vein, which produced 1,515 gallons of water per minute. Very quickly the flow of water coming from the Santa Rita Tunnel ceased. The Virginia and Gold Hill Water Company then leased the water flowing from the Cole Tunnel for about $4 per gallon from the Cole Silver Mining Company. The following year water became so scarce that the water company was forced to supplement their good quality water with Virginia City mine water, mainly from the Ophir Mine shaft.

By 1870, Virginia City and the Comstock had seen several periods of boom and bust as the mines found new ore bodies and then mined them out, going ever deeper on the Comstock Lode, now about 1,000 feet. Between 1864 and 1867 the "Bank of California crowd" and their principals, including William Ralston and William Sharon, had loaned money to mines that couldn't repay the loans. They formed the Union Mill and Mining Company which now controlled most of the mines and mills along the Comstock and were a formidable power. In 1870 their V&T Railroad was completed between Virginia City and Carson City.

The period 1869 through 1870 was one of depression on the Comstock. Ore from the mines was largely low grade and few mines were paying dividends. During this time, John Mackay, James Fair, James Flood, and W.S. O'Brien, known as the "Silver Kings," formed their partnership and took control of the Hale and Norcross Mine from William Sharon. They also bought Sharon's interest in the Virginia and Gold Hill Water Company.

COMPETITION

The Cole Silver Mining Company refused to renew the water company's lease when it expired in 1870. They went into the water business themselves, laying a new system of pipes alongside those of the water company.

The Virginia and Gold Hill Water Company countered by extending the Nevada Tunnel, which was 30 feet lower than the Cole Tunnel. When the Cole Tunnel went dry just as their distribution system was completed, the Cole Silver Mining Company sued the water company in federal court and was granted an injunction in October 1871, stopping the water company from appropriating the water.

Following the ruling the defendant water company bulkheaded the Nevada Tunnel, causing the water to once again flow out of the Cole Tunnel. The Cole Silver Mining Company continued to furnish most of the domestic water to the area, while the Virginia and Gold Hill Water Company continued to furnish water from the mine shafts to the mills in Gold Canyon.

The discovery of a small bonanza ore body in the Crown Point Mine in 1871 revived mining on the Comstock. This revival brought focus to the problems of supplying Virginia City, Gold Hill and the mines and mills of the Comstock with adequate water.

THE IDEA

An idea to transport water to the Comstock from Sierra Creek across Washoe Valley on the east slopes of the Sierra was discussed in the early 1860s, but remained just an idea due to adverse reports from civil engineers who were contacted about the proposed project. They contended that no pipeline had ever been laid with a 1,000 foot head.

The Sierra Nevada bordering the east side of Lake Tahoe with peaks rising from 9,000 to 10,800 feet is a region of heavy precipitation of up to 70 inches per year, mostly snow. Virginia City is about 20 miles to the east and in between are the Eagle and Washoe valleys, some 1,200 to 1,500 feet lower than C Street in Virginia City and some 1,800 feet lower than the Sierra Divide. Separating Eagle Valley (Carson City) and Washoe Valley is a saddle or pass called Lakeview, about 150 feet above Washoe Lake. Water sources in the Sierra were at an elevation high enough to allow a gravity flow, through an inverted siphon, to Virginia City, some 465 feet lower (see diagram on page 48).

The decision to go for Sierra Nevada water was made by the directors of the water company in August 1871 (the "Silver Kings" controlled the water company).

Hermann Schussler, an eminent hydraulic engineer, and also chief engineer of the Spring Valley Water Works of San Francisco, was hired to conduct a feasibility study of the Sierra project. In October 1871, he submitted a favorable report that concluded that water from Hobart Creek could be conveyed through the Sierra in an 18-inch deep flume, enter a pressure pipe to Lakeview Saddle, then up the Virginia Range 6,645 feet in an inverted siphon to another flume which would carry the water to Five Mile Reservoir, where another flume could carry it to Virginia City and Gold Hill. The project was approved and on May 18, 1872 Schussler submitted the specifications and requisition of iron for the pipes. A month later he submitted the specifications and requisition for 952,900 rivets for the pipeline.

LAYING THE FIRST PIPELINE
The pipeline route was surveyed in the spring of 1872 and work began. A small diversion dam was built on Hobart Creek in the Sierra and construction started on the 14.3 miles of wooden flumes that would be required.

Iron for the pipeline was shipped around the Horn from Scotland in 3x10 foot plates to the Risdon Iron and Locomotive Works of San Francisco—the same company that had made most of the iron pipe in use at that time in the hydraulic placer mines of the Mother Lode of California. Using the diagrams of the pipeline route, with elevations, the fabricating company made each section of pipe to fit a certain spot, straight or curved. Fabrication began in March 1873. The thickness of each pipe section varied from 1/16 to 5/16 inches depending upon calculated pressure differences.

The iron plates were cut and rolled into cylinders 26 feet, 2 inches long, with lapping edges allowing for two lines of rivets. All the iron pipe was then coated inside and out with a mixture of asphaltum and coal tar.

The pipe was shipped to Reno on the Central Pacific Railroad, then to Lakeview on the Virginia and Truckee Railroad. The first section of pipe was laid June 11, 1873 and the last of the seven mile section of 12-inch pipeline on July 25 the same year. Considering the very rough terrain, the laying of the pipeline in 2-1/2 to 4 feet deep trenches in six weeks using only mules and manpower was a remarkable feat.

Joints between pipe sections were secured in the field by placing a wrought iron ring around the pipes and filling the space between with lead calking. Altogether some 35 tons of lead were used.

At each place where there was a depression in the pipeline, a blow-off valve was installed for the removal of any sediment. On the top of each ridge an air valve was placed to blow off air when water was first released into the pipeline. This would prevent the collapse of the pipe from vacuum created should a break occur in the pipeline below the air valve.

Water flowed on July 29, but was quickly shut off when leaks from some of the joints occurred because the lead would not hold. All available blacksmiths were recruited to make wrought iron clamps which were placed around each joint with heavy bolts. Repairs were made and, after two more attempts on July 30 and 31 where new leaks were repaired, water was finally again flowing into the pipe at noon on August 1st. A fire and smoke signal marked the event and several anxious hours later water arrived at the outlet end of the pipeline. A beacon fire signifying success was lit for the first time.

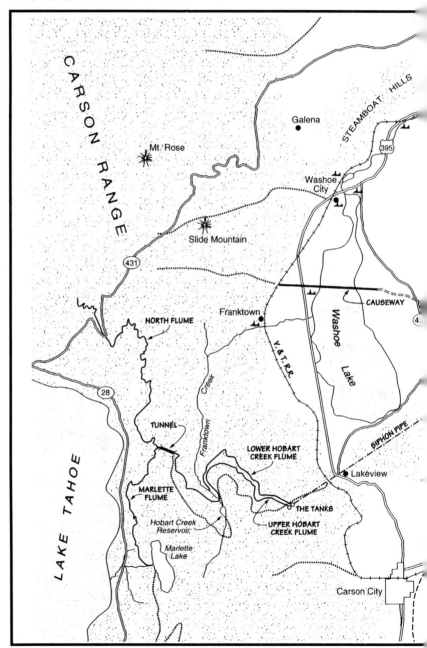

From the outlet of the pressure pipe on the west side of the Virginia Range water entered a four mile long flume which emptied into Five Mile Reservoir at the summit of the range and from the reservoir entered another flume which ran 5.6 miles to Gold Hill and Virginia City. At 6:45 p.m. on August 1, 1873, some 12,000 Comstock residents watched and rejoiced as Sierra water flowed into Bullion Ravine. Two million gallons of water flowed to the Comstock daily.

It was found that in the late summer the water flow from Hobart Creek dropped to about 700,000 gallons per day. With discovery of the Great

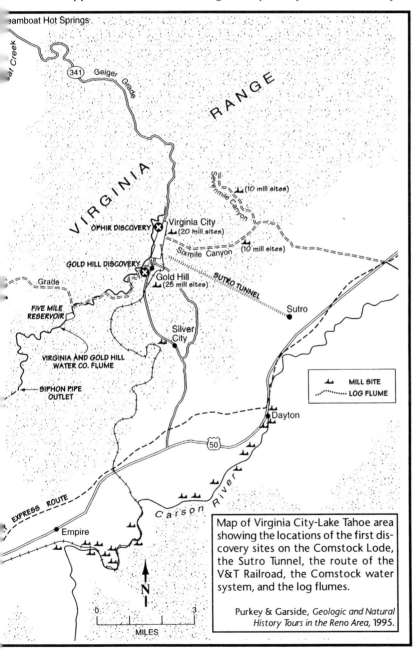

Map of Virginia City-Lake Tahoe area showing the locations of the first discovery sites on the Comstock Lode, the Sutro Tunnel, the route of the V&T Railroad, the Comstock water system, and the log flumes.

Purkey & Garside, *Geologic and Natural History Tours in the Reno Area*, 1995.

Bonanza, activity along the Comstock increased as did the population of Virginia City and Gold Hill and the water usage. More steam was needed in the mines and mills. By 1875, much more water was being used than in 1873, and when the Consolidated Mill started operations in the spring of 1875 the full capacity of the water system was reached: 2,350,000 gallons per day.

THE SECOND PIPELINE

To keep pace with the needs of the Comstock, a second pipeline was started on May 1, 1875 and completed later that year. This pipeline was designed to deliver two million gallons per day, and was welded with screw joints so no rivets were necessary.

To increase the water source area the water company looked to Marlette Lake, a small lake made into a reservoir by the Carson and Tahoe Lumber and Fluming Company which was located on the Lake Tahoe side of the Sierra Summit. The dam was raised and the lake's capacity was increased to two billion gallons. To get the water to Hobart Creek flumes were built and a 3,994 foot tunnel was dug below the Sierra summit. The Divide Tunnel was completed on May 13, 1877. A new reservoir was also built near Hobart Creek with a capacity of 35 million gallons.

By 1878 Virginia City had a population of 25,000 and the V&T Railroad made 32 arrivals and departures daily. Through the next 10 years the Comstock went through boom followed by recession which reached a low in 1881 that lasted until 1887 when production sharply increased. With new activity the demand for additional water increased.

THE THIRD PIPELINE

In 1887 a third pressure pipeline was laid across the Washoe Valley, following the same route as the first two pipes. It was made of lap-welded pipe with converse lock joints.

The entire water supply system now comprised three reservoirs, the three pipelines—two 12-inch and one 10-inch—totalling over 21 miles of pressure pipes, about 46 miles of covered box flumes and the 3,994 foot summit tunnel, capable of delivering seven million gallons of water to the Comstock daily. The distribution system covered the entire Comstock including Virginia City, Gold Hill and Silver City. Water entered a two and one half million gallon reservoir built on the "Divide" between Virginia City and Gold Hill. Each city had a 30,000 gallon wooden tank and there were large storage tanks at many of the mines. There was over 87,000 feet of one to four inch pipes which moved water to the consumers.

About 4.2 million gallons of water was distributed daily, with the mines consuming about two-thirds of the supply. Water rates in 1880 were 20 cents per 1,000 gallons to the mining companies and $4 per month to families of six persons. The total cost of the water system was $2.2 million.

Captain John Overton was Superintendent of the Virginia City and Gold Hill Water Company from 1873 to 1906. He was also Superintendent of the Sierra Nevada Wood and Lumber Company during much of the same time. In 1906 James Leonard became superintendent of the water company.

The water company ownership passed into the Leonard family and then in 1987, to the state of Nevada. Today, the Comstock area is serviced by the second pipeline which provides an average of a little over 200,000 gallons per day.

◆

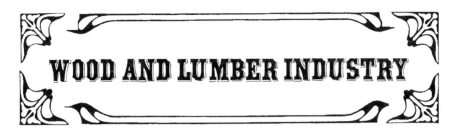

WOOD AND LUMBER INDUSTRY

THE MINING AND ORE REDUCTION ACTIVITIES, along with the building of Virginia City, Gold Hill, Silver City and other nearby communities, required the development of a wood and lumber industry. The results were devastating. The Sierra was stripped of almost all trees from Reno on the north to the headwaters of the Carson River on the south, a distance of 60 miles.

The history of wood and lumber for the Comstock can be divided into three periods. During the first period, 1859-1867, cutting was relatively small scale in the Virginia Range and then along the lower slopes of the Sierra. Second, 1868-1880, the V-flume period, allowed accessibility into remote upper reaches of the Sierra. The third, 1880-1909, marked the decline of the Comstock.

FIRST PERIOD, 1859-1867

The discovery of the Comstock and building of Virginia City required wood for heating stoves and steam boilers; lumber for community construction of buildings, houses and cabins; and timber to be used underground in the mines. The first wood was obtained from the Virginia Range, mainly from piñon pines, and when that was gone, timber was obtained from along the eastern slopes of the Sierra. In 1860, lumber cost $400 per 1,000 feet and native wood from nearby ravines cost $4.25 per cord.

The number of mills rose to 76 by the end of 1861. The machinery for these early mills came from San Francisco, after being shipped around Cape Horn from the east coast. The demand for fuel became so great that several hundred men were cutting and hauling wood from the nearest ravines to the Lode. Wagons brought in loads of wood from the Carson and Washoe valleys. Chinese sold fuel wood for $13 to $30 per cord. Lumber cost $100/thousand plus $200/thousand freight, shipping a distance of 18 miles from the nearest sawmill in the Carson Valley.

Also in 1861, the Ophir Co. built an ore reduction mill along the west side of Washoe Lake, and by 1862 built their own sawmill nearby. The company hauled ore to the mill over a road they constructed called Jumbo Grade, and transported lumber back to their mines on the return trip. The operation lasted two years.

In 1862, a large sawmill was built on the Carson River below Empire, the logs obtained south of Carson City and rafted 80 miles down the East Carson River. About five million board feet were cut annually.

By 1864 there were some 20 predominantly steam-powered sawmills operating within 10 miles of Washoe City, each producing 10,000 feet of lumber daily. Trees were felled by ax and saw. The limbs were trimmed from the trunk which was then cut into 16 to 40 foot lengths. Each year, the turnover of lumberjacks was almost total. The men made small fortunes each season and then left to pursue their dreams.

By 1867, the lower and middle slopes of the east side of the Sierra were denuded and trees were being cut up to the ridge at 9,000 feet. Access roads were expensive because of washout repair costs each spring. Where the grade was very steep, chutes of two parallel lines of logs anchored to the ground were formed, and the big logs slid down to ponds. Square flumes were also used, water being dammed up high in the mountains and the trees washed down the flumes. The logs were then dragged to the mills or transported on large wagons, depending upon distance. The expense of obtaining trees was great.

Every season from 80,000 to 100,000 cords of wood were floated down the Carson River in great "drives" after the spring runoff. French Canadian lumbermen and Paiute Indians were generally used in these drives.

SECOND PERIOD, 1868-1880

The invention of the V-flume by J.W. Harnes in 1866 took two years to perfect. Each section consisted of two boards, each 2 feet wide, 1-1/2 inches thick and 16 feet long. These sections were joined at right angles and underlapped the one above it. It was soon discovered that butt joints properly supported were better. The flumes rested on trestles of variable height and construction with grades of less than one to 20 percent. The flumes needed broad curves to handle 24 to 40 foot long lumber. Water for the main flume was supplied by branches built to adjacent creeks.

With construction of the V-flumes, up to 15 miles in length, the sawmills were relocated higher into the mountains where logs could be readily obtained by teams operating on roads or by log chutes. The flumes transported the lumber and cordwood to the valley floor to large cordwood dumps and lumberyards, from which it was taken to the Comstock by teams and after 1870, by the Virginia & Truckee Railroad.

The demand for lumber increased with discovery of the Crown Point Bonanza in 1871 and the Big Bonanza in the Consolidated Virginia and California mines in 1873. These discoveries stimulated mining throughout the region. With completion of the Central Pacific Railroad to Reno in 1868 and connection with the Virginia and Truckee Railroad in mid-1872, a number of lumber mills were built in the Truckee, California area. These mills would also supply the Comstock with needed cordwood and lumber. The demand continued through 1874 and into 1875. On October 26, 1875 most of Virginia City, along with the hoisting works of the principal mines, burned. The rapid rebuilding required an enormous quantity of lumber.

Lumber would have to be obtained from the highest areas on the eastern slope of Mt. Rose at an elevation of 10,800 feet or from the heavily timbered areas around Lake Tahoe. Three major companies were formed with ample capital to handle larger operations.

The Carson and Tahoe Lumber and Fluming Company was formed in 1873 and operated until 1894. Several of the principals were also part of the Bank of California crowd who also owned the Virginia and Truckee Railroad. At the height of their activities they owned 50,000 acres of timberland on the shores of Lake Tahoe and to the south at Lake Valley. Three mills were operated at Glenbrook, the logs supplied by two steamers on the lake and two logging railroads, with the necessary logging camps. The lumber from the mills was transported to Spooner Summit by wagon and later narrow gauge railroad and then flumed 12 miles down Clear Creek Canyon to a large lumber yard within a mile of Carson City. This yard was serviced by spur tracks of the Virginia & Truckee Railroad.

The milling and logging operations employed as many as 500 men during the eight month season. The wood choppers were mostly French Canadian, Italian and Chinese. The mill crews were imported from Maine.

The Carson and Tahoe Lumber and Fluming Company at Glenbrook was allied with Mills, Ralston and Sharon and the rest of the Bank of California crowd, who were in a power struggle with the "Silver Kings." The "Silver Kings" decided to secure their own source of timber, some 12,000 acres along the eastern slope of the Sierra from about Mt. Rose northward to the Truckee River.

The Pacific Wood, Lumber and Fluming Company was organized in 1875 by the "Silver Kings," Mackay, Fair, Flood and O'Brien. They needed lumber for their mines and they had the financing from their Great Bonanza orebody.

By 1876, a 15-mile flume was built ending near Huffaker's Station on the Virginia and Truckee Railroad line, about 10 miles south of Reno. Two sawmills were built along with 200 miles of mountain roads with the necessary camps for men.

In 1876, about 500 men were employed, delivering 15 million board feet of lumber and 75,000 cords of wood at Huffaker's.

The third major company, the Sierra Nevada Wood and Lumber Company, was organized in 1878 and operated in the Lake Tahoe area until 1896. Its principals were tied to the Virginia Water Works. A steam-powered sawmill was completed in 1880 on Mill Creek, about one mile east of what is now Incline Village. Timber was obtained along the northern slope of Lake Tahoe and rafted to Sand Harbor and then hauled by a narrow gauge railroad to the mill. Lumber and cordwood were hauled by a 4,000 foot-long double-track tramway (Incline) 1,400 feet up the mountain where it was transferred to a V-flume which was built through the 3,994-foot water company tunnel. It then dropped eastward about 2,500 feet in elevation down the mountain to a lumber yard at Lakeview, where the Virginia & Truckee Railroad crossed on its trip to the Comstock.

Records of shipments by the Virginia and Truckee Railroad for the period 1874 through 1879, show 1.14 million cords of fuel wood and 301.2 million board feet of lumber moved to the Comstock.

In 1880, there were 20 flumes along the eastern Sierra front, over 80 miles in total length, transporting annually 171,000 cords of wood and 33.3 million board feet of lumber.

The total timber used in the mines through 1880 is estimated at 450 million board feet.

THIRD PERIOD, 1880-1909
This period marked the declining years of the Comstock. There was much deep exploration yielding few new ore bodies. Most of the ore mined was low grade through about 1895.

About $40 million was spent between 1880 and 1886 in deep exploration but little ore was found.

Virginia City's population in 1880 was about 11,000. This dwindled to 2,700 by 1900 and continued downward.

Two of the three major companies continued to operate through the 1880s. The Carson and Tahoe Lumber and Fluming Company shut down in 1894, and their Lake Valley Railroad to Spooner Summit was abandoned in 1898. The Sierra Nevada Wood and Lumber Company shut down operations in 1896, moving their mill and rail equipment to Hobart Mills, north of Truckee, California.

SUMMARY
From 1860 to 1880 the total lengths of underground workings along the four miles of the Comstock Lode is estimated at 190 miles which consumed

about 450 million board feet of timber, most commonly sawed square, 12x12 inches, which included about 150 million board feet of 14 and 16 inch square-set timbers.

Total wood for fuel for the mines and mills is estimated to be near two million cords.

As the population of the area fell away, abandoned houses were torn down and used for fuel.

Today, the tourists who walk the streets of Virginia City walk over a forest of underground timbers of mammoth dimensions, most of which were obtained from the Sierra.

The Virginia Range and the Sierra now have new growth of piñon and pine trees, except in areas of recent fires, which cover the areas stripped by logging during the Comstock era. There are still remnants of flumes, mills, camps and roads visible in places.

◆

GOLD HILL CIRCA 1860s.
Courtesy of Nevada Historical Society.

JOINT SHAFT OF THE CHOLLAR, POTOSI, HALE & NORCROSS AND SAVAGE MINING COMPANIES (COMBINATION SHAFT) CIRCA 1860s.
Courtesy of Nevada Historical Society.

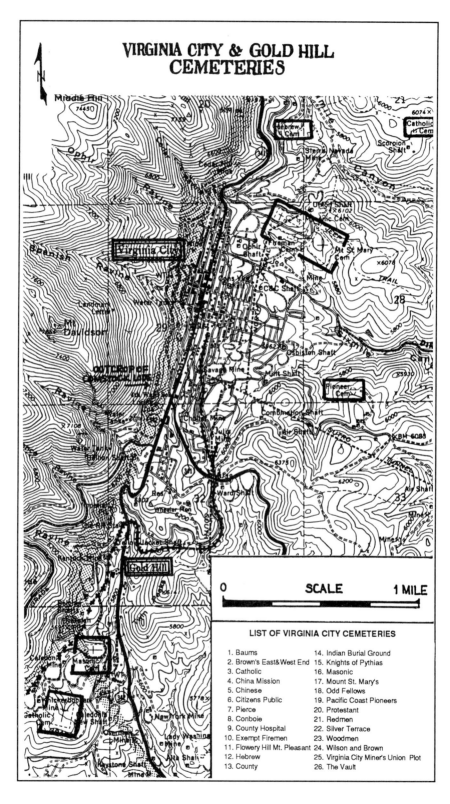

VIRGINIA CITY & GOLD HILL CEMETERIES

SCALE 0 — 1 MILE

LIST OF VIRGINIA CITY CEMETERIES

1. Baums
2. Brown's East&West End
3. Catholic
4. China Mission
5. Chinese
6. Citizens Public
7. Pierce
8. Conboie
9. County Hospital
10. Exempt Firemen
11. Flowery Hill Mt. Pleasant
12. Hebrew
13. County
14. Indian Burial Ground
15. Knights of Pythias
16. Masonic
17. Mount St. Mary's
18. Odd Fellows
19. Pacific Coast Pioneers
20. Protestant
21. Redmen
22. Silver Terrace
23. Woodmen
24. Wilson and Brown
25. Virginia City Miner's Union Plot
26. The Vault

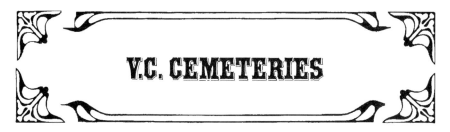

V.C. CEMETERIES

IN MOST OLD WESTERN MINING CAMPS built between 1850 and 1900, residents were extremely rigid in the belief that their cemeteries should be completely segregated by religion, fraternal order, nationality, and ethnic and racial background. Prejudice was the norm of that time. Indians (Native Americans), Mexicans, Chinese, and Jews were not allowed to be buried near Christian Americans and Europeans. The Virginia City cemeteries were no exception.

Very little has been written about the Virginia City cemeteries and with few old maps available, their history must be pieced together. Two of the earliest cemeteries (early 1860s) are the Pioneer Cemetery found in the southwest corner of Section 28, just east of where the old county hospital stood (about where the "P" of Pioneer appears on the map east of Virginia City), and the Catholic Cemetery near the center of Section 21, about one mile northeast of Virginia City.

Little has been done to maintain the Pioneer Cemetery. Outlines of a few graves can be seen from the decayed old wood fencing. A chain link fence and marker shows where some believe Julia Bulette, notorious "lady of the evening," is buried, but this is questionable. The same is true for the Catholic Cemetery. All that remains are remnants of wooden fences that surrounded the graves.

The Hebrew Cemetery was established in the early 1860s by the Eureka Society and can be seen a few hundred yards east of Highway 341 about one third mile north of Virginia City along the east edge of Section 20. This cemetery is also in a state of disrepair, although periodically maintained.

Virginia City had a substantial Chinese population but where they were buried is not known. Some old time Virginia City residents claim to know where old Chinese graves are located but will not divulge the information. Others suggest that a Chinese burial ground was located south of Six Mile Canyon and east of the Pioneer Cemetery. It was the custom at that time for affluent Chinese to remove family remains about a year after death and take them back to China for reburial.

The "Mercantile Guide and Directory for Virginia City, Gold Hill, and Silver City," published by Charles Collins in 1864-65, states that, "a tract of 27 acres located on Flowery Hill was purchased for $2,500 by the city from J.B. Wallard for use as a cemetery. As best as can be determined the 27 acres were divided into at least nine separate cemeteries as shown on the map on pages 62-63.

St. Mary's Catholic Cemetery, with its large cross, was probably established in 1863-64 just east of the main cemeteries. This cemetery was under the charge of Reverend Father Manogue and had about 100 buried in it by 1865.

Although most of the early wood markers have long rotted, many of the headstones are still standing along with metal fencing. Walking through the main cemeteries, one notices the great number of immigrants from the British Empire and Europe, the Civil War veterans, the young mothers, babies and children buried here. Many of the deaths were from disease and infection during childbirth.

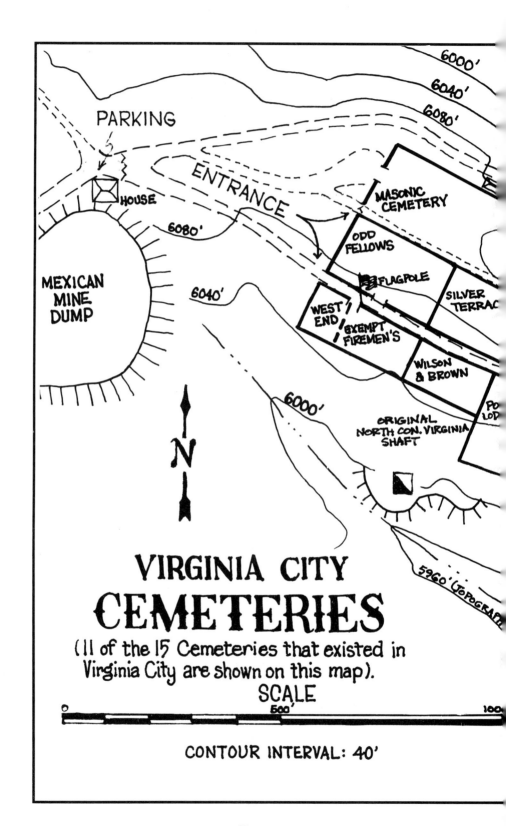

PARKING

HOUSE

ENTRANCE

6000'

6040'

6080'

MASONIC CEMETERY

ODD FELLOWS

6080'

MEXICAN MINE DUMP

6040'

FLAGPOLE

SILVER TERRAC

WEST END

EXEMPT FIREMEN'S

WILSON & BROWN

PO LOD

6000'

ORIGINAL NORTH CON. VIRGINIA SHAFT

N

5960' (TOPOGRAPH

VIRGINIA CITY
CEMETERIES

(II of the I5 Cemeteries that existed in Virginia City are shown on this map).

SCALE

0   500'   100

CONTOUR INTERVAL: 40'

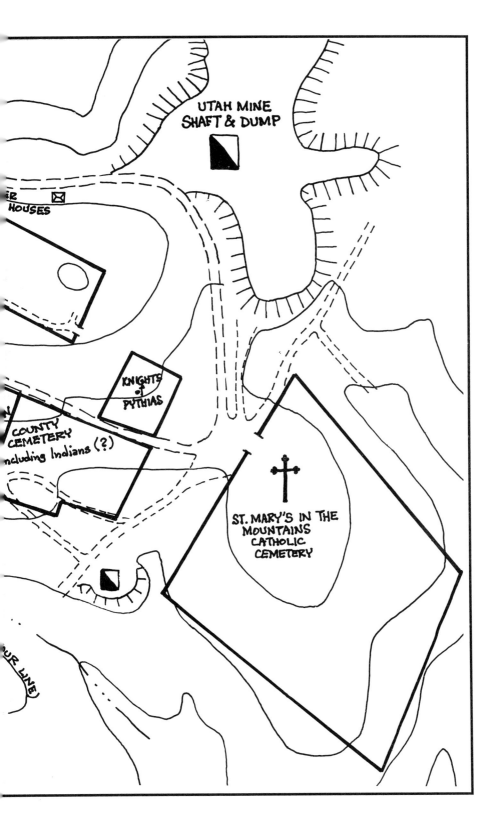

UTAH MINE
SHAFT & DUMP

HOUSES

KNIGHTS
PYTHIAS

COUNTY
CEMETERY
including Indians (?)

ST. MARY'S IN THE
MOUNTAINS
CATHOLIC
CEMETERY

UR LINE)

REFERENCES

Becker, George F., "Geology of the Comstock Lode and the Washoe District — with Atlas," United States Geological Survey, 1882.

Beebe, Lucius and Charles Clegg, *Steamcars to the Comstock,* Howell-North Books, Berkeley, California, 1957.

Beebe, Lucius and Charles Clegg, *Virginia and Truckee — A Story of Virginia City and Comstock Times,* Nevada State Railroad Museum, 7th Edition, 1991.

Davis, Sam P. (Ed.), *The History of Nevada, Volume I,* Illustrated, The Elms Publishing Co., Reno, Nevada, 1913.

Galloway, John Delio, "Early Engineering Works Contributory to the Comstock," University of Nevada Bulletin, Geology and Mining Series, Nevada State Bureau of Mines, No. 45, Vol. 41, No. 5, June 1947.

Myrick, David F., *Railroads of Nevada and Eastern California,* Vol. 1, Howell North Books, Berkeley, California, 1962.

Shamberger, Hugh A., *The Story of the Water Supply for the Comstock—1859-1969,* Historic Mining Camps of Nevada Series, No. 1, Nevada Historical Press, Carson City, Nevada, 1972; United States Geological Survey Professional Paper 779, 1972.

Smith, Grant H., "The History of the Comstock Lode 1850-1920," University of Nevada Bulletin, Geology and Mining Series, Nevada Bureau of Mines and Geology, No. 37, Vol. 37, No. 3, July 1943.

Stewart, Robert E. Jr. and Mary Frances Stewart, *Adolph Sutro — A Biography,* Howell North Books, Berkeley, California, 1962.

Sutro, Theodore, "The Sutro Tunnel Company and Sutro Tunnel — Report to the Stockholders," New York, July 1887.

Wurm, Ted and Harre W. Demoro, *The Silver Shortline — A History of the V&T RR,* Trans-Anglo Books, Glendale, California, 1983.